The Great Nonprofit Evaluation Reboot

A New Approach Every Staff Member Can Understand

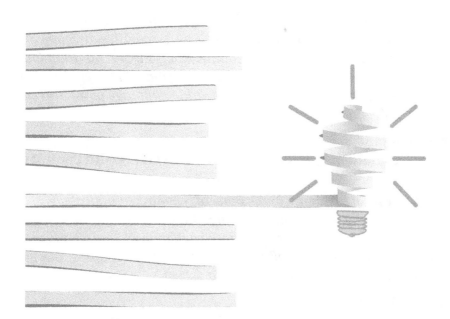

Elena Harman, PhD

What Others Are Saying...

Elena Harman has put together an excellent and user-friendly guidebook about evaluation for nonprofits that takes the fear out of measurement and makes it accessible for any nonprofit professional. This is important because using an evaluation is the only way nonprofits can know if their programs are effective and they are truly changing the world.

Beth Kanter
Speaker, Author, and Master Trainer

I've been working in the nonprofit field for nearly twenty years. In that time, I've worn many hats, including executive director, communications manager, development person, and board member. Elena's advice on how evaluation can contribute to the effectiveness of each one of these roles, as well as the unique vantage point that each plays in effective evaluation, is both insightful and practical.

Amy Latham
Vice President of Philanthropy, The Colorado Health Foundation

Elena Harman brilliantly covers one of the most complicated tasks that funders and nonprofits face: how to evaluate both those who make grants and those who receive them. Her complete and friendly book presents a solid path to evaluation without strain and frustration.

Martin Teitel
Author of *The Ultimate Insider's Guide to Winning Foundation Grants: A Foundation CEO Reveals the Secrets You Need to Know*

Evaluation is a critical component of running effective programs, as well as raising more money for those programs. If you want to provide the best services possible, and communicate that with your donors, this book is a must read.

Amy Eisenstein, ACFRE
Speaker, Consultant, and Author of *Major Gift Fundraising for Small Shops*

Elena's chapter for fundraisers offers essential evaluation methods that development officers can easily apply. Full of fresh perspectives for individual, foundation, and corporate donors, Elena recommends evaluating fundraising channels such as online campaigns and direct mail to test your messaging and formatting—my own refrain for many years. I especially appreciated her focus on educating donors about what data to ask for and why, as well as how important discoveries can help you deepen donor relationships and interactions—whether at your gala or simply over coffee.

Deborah Polivy
Author of *The Donor Lifecycle Map: A Model for Fundraising Success*

Music to my ears: Elena tells us "don't talk metrics—talk about what matters." Yes! Just imagine "evaluation as a learning tool rather than an accountability measure." Great! Use this book to make sure that your programs advance mission. This book effectively sets the context for program evaluation and provides hands-on tools. Use with staff and board. Read it now!

Simone Joyaux, ACFRE
Firing Lousy Board Members: And Helping the Others Succeed

What an amazing resource for the nonprofit sector. This book helped me see evaluation in a new light—as a learning process, not an accountability tool. And it opened my eyes not only to ways in which evaluation can support communications, but also the role of the communication team in supporting evaluation. With rich examples, helpful tips, and a down-to-earth writing style, I feel this book is a treasure trove of actionable steps that will inspire readers to start implementing great ideas right away. I especially love the insights into what social media metrics we should really care about and the honest assessment of when it does and does not make sense to evaluate. What a gift!

Jami Fassett
Founder and Chief Brand Strategist of Up & Up Creative

The Great Nonprofit Evaluation Reboot: A New Approach Every Staff Member Can Understand

Elena Harman, PhD

Published by
CharityChannel Press, an imprint of CharityChannel LLC
PO Box 14
Pleasant View, TN 37146-0014 USA

CharityChannel.com

ISBN Print Book: 978-1-938077-92-0

Library of Congress Control Number: 2018967194

13 12 11 10 9 8 7 6 5 4 3 2 1

Printed in the United States of America

This and most CharityChannel Press books are available at special quantity discounts for bulk purchases for sales promotions, premiums, fundraising, or educational use. For information, contact CharityChannel Press, PO Box 14, Pleasant View, TN 37146-0014 USA. +1 949-589-5938.

Publisher's Acknowledgments

This book was produced by a team dedicated to excellence; please send your feedback to Editors@CharityChannel.com.

We first wish to acknowledge the tens of thousands of peers who call *CharityChannel.com* their online professional home. Your enthusiastic support for CharityChannel Press is the wind in our sails.

Members of the team who produced this book include:

Editors

Acquisitions: Denise McMahan

Manuscript Editing: Stephen Nill

Production

Cover and Interior Design: Stephen Nill

Layout: Stephen Nill

Administrative

CharityChannel LLC: Stephen Nill, CEO

Marketing and Public Relations: John Millen

About the Author

Elena Harman, PhD, is the CEO and Founder of Vantage Evaluation, a consulting firm committed to evolving the way purpose-driven nonprofits think about and use evaluation—from data for data's sake to evaluation as a learning process, guiding strategic improvements. Elena's expertise lies in maintaining the big-picture view of how evaluation can inform high-quality social programming and engaging diverse audiences in a productive conversation about evaluation. Prior to launching Vantage Evaluation in 2013, Elena was an internal evaluator at the Colorado Health Foundation, where she helped launch the foundation's measurable results evaluation model. Elena holds a BS in Brain and Cognitive Sciences from M.I.T. and an MA and PhD in Evaluation and Applied Research Methods from Claremont Graduate University. Her work has been published in the journal *Evaluation and Program Planning*. She is a regular presenter at nonprofit conferences throughout Colorado and served as the president of the Colorado Evaluation Network in 2019.

Dedication

To the Vantage team, who bring these ideas to life every day.

Author's Acknowledgments

This book is the result of an incredible network of people who supported my lifetime of learning, thinking, and creating. Thank you to my family, Nea, David, and Jay, who encouraged my attendance at varied and unusual academic institutions, cultivated a love of big ideas, and never refused the purchase of another book. Tobie Weiner at M.I.T., who set me on the path that would lead me to evaluation. My mentors at the Colorado Health Foundation, most of all Alexis Weightman, Marisa Allen, and Shepard Nevel. The professors at Claremont Graduate University, particularly Tarek Azzam, Tiffany Berry, Stewart Donaldson, and Michael Scriven, who held space for me to learn from evaluation greats and shape my own perspectives. Other evaluation firm owners and operators who have been generous in sharing their hard-earned expertise are Komani Lundquist, Corey Newhouse, Leah Goldstein Moses, Nishi Moonka, Clare Nolan, Jewlya Lynn, and Kirk Knestis. And Kelci Price, a friend, colleague, and connector, reassuring me that I could make a difference in the evaluation field at just the right times.

None of my work would be possible without my team at Vantage Evaluation. Kayla Brooks, Morgan Cook, Stacie Hanson, Aisha Rios, Laura Sundstrom, and Morgan Valley, thank you. Each member of the team played a critical role in developing these ideas, testing them in our evaluation practice, and taking on a heavier workload so I could focus on writing.

This book would not have come to be without the encouragement of a stranger, Anthony Graves, who told me that I should write it. I am forever grateful to Denise McMahan for taking on my writing and helping edit and format its way into a book. And to Stephen Nill and his team at CharityChannel Press for bringing it to print. I'd also like to thank Ted Hart for inspiring the title of this book.

And lastly, I want to thank my husband, Cole Kauffman. Though he insists he will never read the final product, he supported the development of this book in countless ways.

Contents

Summary of Chapters

Disconnected: The Evaluation Field and Nonprofits We Serve. The evaluation field's journey over the years has affected our perceptions and realities about the client and evaluator relationship. I explain my misgivings about counterproductive practices in evaluation and share my vision for healthier client-evaluator partnerships and their profound benefits.

Why Evaluation Needs a Reboot. While there have been great strides over the years in the evaluation field, it has also experienced its share of missteps, particularly with academics and career evaluators who persist in using hurdles like jargon and focusing on rigor instead of accessibility. The result is often a chasm between what the social sector needs and what the evaluation field thinks it needs.

Shifting Our Mindset. This chapter is about readiness. I call on the field of evaluation and the social sector to shift entrenched thinking, so clients and consultants can engage in evaluation as equals with a focus on engagement rather than alienation. These shifts are finding common ground in concepts, orienting toward learning and increasing our focus on usability.

Breaking It Down. If you're considering evaluation for your programs, the first step is often the most difficult. So, I break down the five core elements of effective evaluation one by one. Think of these core elements as the backbone, or spine for the sake of my later metaphor, of effective evaluation. By the end of the section, you have a better understanding of how to get started and how to effectively measure your outcomes.

Getting Clarity So You Can Map Your Program. Now that you've entertained a different mindset, I explain how to get clarity about what you'd like to evaluate. To do that, we first articulate what your program does and is trying to achieve. Next, I share my field-tested approach to help you create a program map and bridge the gap between program planning, evaluation planning, and your purpose statement.

Creating Great Questions to Guide Your Evaluation. If you earmark one chapter about evaluation, this is it. I outline a framework for explaining the most important things you want to learn from evaluation. By the end, you'll understand different questions and how to structure them, plus some insider tips.

Choosing the Right Methods to Answer Your Questions. Together, we explore which evaluation approaches are best for different types of key evaluation questions. I walk you through the differences between quantitative and qualitative data and the advantages of using both. We close with some tips on how to know which data sources are best for your questions.

Executing the Evaluation. At this point, we transition toward the actual execution of the evaluation. In this chapter, we examine the critical considerations for implementation in the real world no matter what methods you are using. For example, we discuss designing instruments, collecting data, and analyzing that data. I also cover common questions, pitfalls, and logistical considerations.

Getting the Most out of Reflection. We start with a discussion of how to make your written evaluation results as impactful as possible in this chapter. Then we move into how to discuss them internally at your nonprofit and, finally, we conclude with tips on sharing evaluation results externally.

Pick Your Position: How Evaluation Can Work for You. Carrying out evaluation cuts across the entire organizational chart and needs the engagement of every staff member. This section explains how each position can uniquely apply evaluation techniques to amplify results. I introduce the body's head and limbs as a metaphor to explain how programs require the animation of all body parts to move evaluation forward.

The Executive Director. Since executive directors—the metaphorical head in our evaluation body—wear the most hats, we discuss their role in evaluation first. This chapter presents the nonprofit Love Over Hate to explore the challenges and choices surrounding the task of internalizing, embedding, staffing, and communicating evaluation.

The Communications Team. The communications team represents the first arm in our evaluation body. Through the lens of the nonprofit Businesses Unite we consider events and conferences, reports and publications, and social media in the realm of communications. Then we discuss how the team can support messaging that's focused on learning, contribution not attribution, and closing the feedback loop with beneficiaries.

The Development Team. The development position represents the second arm in our evaluation body, reaching out to its funders with relevant data for each constituency: grants, individuals, and corporations. We take a look at the nonprofit Books for All and how it engaged foundations with a results-rich approach, as well as explore essential topics like how to tackle tricky grant questions.

The Board of Directors. The board of directors, the evaluation body's leg, can mobilize your nonprofit, which makes its support and encouragement of evaluation essential to growth and stability. This chapter introduces the nonprofit Education to Action, which tells an enlightening board story and prepares you for topics such as asking productive questions, interacting with results, and sharing the data.

Foundations. Foundations couldn't have a more fitting limb in our body metaphor because the nonprofit in this chapter, Healthy Huerfano, applied extensive legwork to move its mission forward. This chapter explores how a foundation can evaluate itself and the impact of its grantees. I also explain how foundations can join the movement in sharing their good and bad results.

Let's Get Started. This section of the book prepares you to apply the discussions we've had so far in **Part Two,** which provides a necessary framework, or as we explained, the backbone, for effective evaluation. Then **Part Three** explores all the moving parts or positions that activate evaluation. This last portion of the book assembles and cross-references content I think is helpful for making those early steps.

Bringing It All Together. This chapter recognizes the connections we can draw between all of the subject matter we've covered together. Now your nonprofit looks different and, as a result, can be different, can think strategically, and can fund itself incrementally. We revisit some collective themes by turning back to Books for All and share a Nonprofit Evaluation Bill of Rights.

Taking the First Step. Though this chapter is called "Taking the First Step," I'm sure it may feel a little bit more like a leap! Not to worry; this closing is designed to let you choose a leap that's within your comfort zone. I list three options for getting started, including the "Goldilocks" of options that may feel just right. Enjoy the adventure!

Foreword

If you've picked up this book, chances are you have at least a passing interest in evaluation and how it can be used to make your work more effective. Perhaps you've come to this book out of a sense of dissatisfaction with how evaluation has worked—or not—to improve your nonprofit's programs or services. Or maybe you are ready to lead a conversation within your organization about how evaluation can increase the impact of your nonprofit in your community.

Unfortunately for many folks working in the social sector, the word "evaluation" conjures negative reactions—worries about finger-pointing, concerns about funder reactions, or fear of negative public perceptions if the results aren't all positive. Deciding to evaluate your program's effectiveness, and then figuring out how to do it, can be a daunting proposition. But it shouldn't be. It's the simple act of asking what's working, what's not working, and why. It can lead to profound insights and, ultimately, improvements to our work that increase the impact we are having in the communities we are here to serve. Who wouldn't want to take part in that? How different would our world be if we all used the approach that Elena Harman advocates here—asking ourselves smart questions, thoughtfully aligning our approaches to answering those questions, and then collectively using the information that we gather to make informed decisions for improvements? Reading this book has affirmed my belief in, and ignited my passion for, evaluation as a tool for increasing impact.

I've been working in the nonprofit field for nearly twenty years. In that time, I've worn many hats, including executive director, communications manager, development person, and board member. Elena's advice on how evaluation can contribute to the effectiveness of each one of these roles, as well as the unique vantage point that each plays in effective evaluation, is both insightful and practical. For the last ten years, I've worked at a health foundation that is fortunate enough to have a wonderful evaluation team whose members serve as critical learning partners to the program staff. I've come to understand that I've been fortunate in my experience with evaluation and that much of the field is stuck in the accountability frame that Elena advocates against so articulately in this book. The field of nonprofit evaluation is evolving in positive ways. Nothing, however, is quite the breath of fresh air as Elena's unequivocal call to shift the frame of evaluation from one of accountability to learning. She offers simple tips that provide easy ways to get started no matter your role or your experience with evaluation.

I had the pleasure of working with Elena when she was fresh out of college—excited about her role as an evaluator at the foundation we worked for and brimming with enthusiasm and ideas for how we could use data to improve our work. At that time, I recognized but didn't fully understand Elena's passion for evaluation. Flash forward eight years, and I'm sitting in a room with Elena, who now owns her own business. She is helping our foundation team examine the impact of our funding in the area of access to primary care. Light bulbs are going off for me right and left as I digest the "data sandwiches" that Elena and her team have developed. I'm thinking of ways we can apply what we learned to our work going forward, and I cannot wait to share the results with other staff, with my boss, with our board. Because we sat together with Elena and her team to develop the evaluation questions, there was not just interest, but a hunger for the data that her team would find. The approach absolutely guaranteed that the evaluation data would be used by our team in trying to improve our funding approaches.

Here's why this book is so critical: communities are facing serious, urgent issues on a variety of fronts, and nonprofits cannot afford to waste time, resources, and energy. We need to know what's working; we need to identify ways that we can improve; and we need to be doing this all the time, on an ongoing basis. It's in that spirit that Elena offers a guide that anyone working in the nonprofit sector could pick up, read in a couple of hours, and start putting to use immediately. It's a small investment in the effectiveness and impact of the work we do, but well worth it.

Amy Latham
Vice President of Philanthropy
The Colorado Health Foundation

Introduction

Changing the Conversation About Evaluation

My first conversation with a nonprofit typically goes a little a bit like this:

Nonprofit: *I want to evaluate my program.*

Elena: *That's great! Tell me a little bit more about what you want to evaluate.*

Nonprofit: *My program.*

Elena: *Okay...*

The seemingly harmless phrase, "I want to evaluate my program," can spell disaster for nonprofits that jump from there right into evaluation. Without more specificity, it's unlikely that the evaluation you end up with will address what you care about. Two components of this short phrase are problematic:

My Program: In your corner of the universe, you have a really clear understanding of what your nonprofit and program do and what you're trying to achieve. But the degree to which other staff members within your nonprofit, let alone board members and participants, share that understanding, varies. "My program" can mean something different to every individual who touches the program.

And if you don't clarify up front what exactly is being evaluated, interpreting the results after the fact gets complicated quickly. Say you learn that "the program" is a rock star, achieving everything you'd hoped for and more.

You now want to duplicate the program at other sites. But when you move forward with planning, it turns out that each of the existing program sites operates differently! Which program was the rock star? Do you expand one version in full or the pieces that all programs have in common? Clarity about what program you are evaluating at the outset avoids these questions that are all but unanswerable after the fact.

To Evaluate: "I want to evaluate" implies that evaluation looks the same in different contexts and in different settings. And an evaluator is an evaluator, right? Not quite. Evaluation is a single word for a field with countless approaches and philosophies that yield different evaluation products through dramatically different processes. It's a bit like saying you need a lawyer without specifying which kind. Do you need a tax attorney or a criminal defense attorney? Each evaluator you interact with was trained in a different specialty within the field and brings a unique set of biases and standard operating procedures.

If you don't articulate at the beginning what you are hoping to learn, again, with specificity, the decision will be made for you. The decision often defaults to the perspective of the internal or external evaluators you hire and the type of evaluation in which they were trained. Don't leave this to chance. If you care most about gaining a detailed understanding of how beneficiaries experience your program, and you hire an evaluator who specializes in using quantitative experimental approaches to understand the long-term impact of programs, you'll be left with an empty bank account and an evaluation without practical relevance to your work.

After nearly a decade in the evaluation field, the number one pitfall I have seen is not taking the time at the start of an evaluation to get clear about these two things. Without clear explication of what you are evaluating and why, evaluation turns into collecting data for data's sake, without any valuable insights at the end. It breaks my heart because it doesn't have to be this way.

My Backstory

Before I get started on my views about evaluation, let me give you some backstory on my formative years in the field and how those experiences shaped my hopes for the profession. I fell into the evaluation field immediately after I graduated from college. While in college, I experimented with potential career paths, none of which fit me quite right. With graduation on the horizon, I started having conversations with professionals in my hometown of Denver about what might be next for me.

I got lucky. I sat at a coffee shop with Annie, whose children I'd babysat as a teenager, and described what I was looking for:

> I need a career that gives back to my community, but direct service was not a good fit for me. I tried policy work, and that was closer intellectually, but it was too far removed from my community—I'd miss data and the scientific process if I get too far away from that. And my interest in serving the community is broad. There is not one topic, like health care or the environment that I could dedicate my life to. I guess I want to do something that helps all direct service work be really, really effective.

"What you are describing," Annie responded, "is called evaluation, and it's what you should be doing for the rest of your life."

From there, I was off to the races. Annie knew about evaluation because she worked at the largest health foundation in the state of Colorado as it was beginning to build out an evaluation department. The foundation took a chance on me and hired me out of college as the second member of a two-person team charged with implementing its evaluation model. I fell in love with evaluation fast and hard. This was what I had been looking for! It had the intellectual challenge of basic scientific research with the interpersonal challenge of policy work and the feeling like I could really change the world of direct service. I was regularly spotted skipping down the hallways with spreadsheets of data I wanted to share with one program officer or another, and while the rest of the staff found my antics amusing, there was a general lack of interest from my coworkers in the things that excited me.

Why wouldn't the program officers get as excited about statistical significance as I did? Didn't they understand how cool it was? This was my first experience with the gap between evaluators and the people and nonprofits that evaluators work in service of. In the times when I was not skipping down the halls with data, my role at the foundation was primarily managing evaluation contractors, supporting grantees' attempts to meet our new evaluation reporting requirements, and spending 90 percent of my time in meetings trying to help program staff think about and use evaluation. Huh, I thought. If the foundation, with ample resources and executive commitment to evaluation, needs internal staff to translate between evaluation speak and program speak, what do nonprofits and smaller foundations do about evaluation? How can we bring nonprofits and evaluators in closer partnership, so evaluation can live up to its potential as the indispensable strategic tool I know it can be?

I decided to try to find out, venturing off to graduate school to get my PhD in evaluation and applied research methods. If anyone had this figured out, it'd be the top theorists and researchers in the evaluation field. In graduate school, I found the people who got excited about the same things I did. We could nerd out for hours about the minute details of technical methodology or differences in approach of our evaluation theory idols. If any of my former coworkers could have heard our conversations, their eyes would have glazed over immediately. I loved learning the ins and outs of the evaluation field and its history, and it became clear to me in graduate school that evaluation could be a powerful strategic tool for nonprofits. I saw examples in the projects my professors ran.

They supported high-quality implementation of after-school programming and helped college access programs figure out why programming that worked in Michigan didn't work in Los Angeles. But I also realized that academia was not my world either. In between the exemplars of evaluation practice, the jargon and ingrained power dynamics made most of the evaluation work I learned about just as removed from community nonprofits as my role at the foundation. Instead of feeling like the evaluator out of place in the nonprofit world, I felt like the nonprofit staff out of place in the evaluator world.

I wanted to find a world where the two merge—where evaluators and nonprofits spoke the same language and worked toward the same goal of strengthening our communities. In the world I was searching for, evaluation served our communities through nonprofits' needs, not through their funders' need. My dream evaluation focused on the unanswered questions that mattered most to nonprofit staff. Rather than tunnel vision on specific research outcomes, the evaluation I pictured focused on the questions that would help nonprofit staff do their jobs better.

What's more, I envisioned evaluation changing from a tool to hold nonprofits accountable to a learning process, helping program staff understand what works, what doesn't, and how to improve services over time. In my version of events, we'd use the best methods available to answer those questions, within the constraints of the everyday reality and resource limitations of nonprofit work. And we'd present the results in a way that nonprofit staff could immediately understand and digest. The evaluation I was searching for did not tell programs what to do but spoke for the data and let nonprofit staff interpret what action items that data suggested. The evaluation I dreamt of was a partnership between nonprofit and evaluator, with the evaluation ultimately and authentically in service of helping the nonprofit do its work better.

In reality, I've found pockets of this world scattered throughout the evaluation field, but it's not yet universal. Conversation by conversation and project by project, I'm on a mission to craft an evaluation world in service of our communities and the nonprofits that touch them. I want to change the conversation about evaluation so that it is less about isolated instances of collecting data for data's sake and more about a strategic learning process woven into the day-to-day fabric of nonprofits. We should think of evaluation as part of programs, not separate from programs. Evaluation should be first and foremost about a thinking process and second about technical methodologies. And the role of evaluators should be to support this process as a thought partner, not to descend upon nonprofits as "the expert."

But right now, the support available to nonprofits about evaluation are heavily slanted toward the doing of evaluation and the technical methodologies. For instance, the resources are bent on how to design a survey and how to analyze qualitative data instead of the thinking of evaluation. In fact, I have found very few resources about evaluation for the nonprofits that we purport to serve. Evaluators love to write books for other evaluators, and you can find textbook after textbook filled with technical details about evaluation. But what about support and resources for consumers of evaluation, focusing on how they can engage effectively with evaluation and position themselves for success?

That's where this book fits in. My hope is to break the pattern of expecting non-evaluators on the nonprofit team to make use of resources written for evaluators. This book is just for you. For the nonprofit staff member without formal evaluation training who suddenly finds evaluation has become a part of the job. For the board member who just learned the term *evaluation* and is looking for a place to start. For the executive director who knows that evaluation is a best practice but can't figure out why, because it's never seemed useful before. This book aims to support your engagement with evaluation, show you the world that I dream of, and suggest some incremental steps to get us there. So, let's take a look inside.

How This Book Is Organized

The book is broken up into four parts. In **Part One,** we'll set the stage for where we find ourselves today by discussing what the current conversation about evaluation is missing. We will talk about how the evaluation field came to be the way it is today. And we'll explore how we can break the pattern and together create a world where nonprofits and evaluators work as equals to strengthen our communities.

Part Two outlines the five steps of evaluation. The first three steps, mapping your program, articulating key evaluation questions, and matching your questions to methods, cover evaluation planning. The fourth step is to execute the evaluation, followed by reflecting on and learning from the findings. Only steps three and four require any technical knowledge. The rest is just putting structure to a thought process.

After you finish **Part Two,** the paths diverge: **Part Three** contains a chapter specific to five core nonprofit positions. Because as hard as we try to make it fit into one job description, evaluation cuts across nonprofit roles. The development staff person has to talk about it with funders, the executive director has to staff it, and the board of directors has to support it. We will talk through how executive directors, development staff, communications staff, the board of directors, and foundations can most effectively engage with and support evaluation efforts. Pick the chapter that applies best to you and start there, though you might find nuggets in chapters for other positions as well since we know that one's workload tends to spill over into another. Finally, we end the book with **Part Four,** bringing everyone back together. First, we'll talk about how all the chapters in **Part Two** and **Part Three** come together. And then we'll share some suggestions about where to get started.

I pack each chapter with actionable tips and real-life stories of nonprofits that have implemented them. Each case story represents a blend of client characteristics I've worked with in the past to give you a rich understanding of evaluation. I've also used pseudonyms in place of actual client names. The sidebars throughout this book contain personal observations, guidance, and examples that add insights into my prescriptive advice. Ultimately, my goal is not that you immediately implement everything we talk about when you finish this book. Rather, I hope you will find a few strategies that resonate with you and use those as an entry point to implementing evaluation efforts that truly serve your strategic process. And of course, that you will find evaluators—whether on your staff or external contractors— who can partner with you in this effort.

Part One

Disconnected: The Evaluation Field and the Nonprofits We Serve

While evaluation has been in the nonprofit vocabulary for years and often with a negative connotation, it's not always clear how evaluation rose to prominence and why it doesn't feel quite right to nonprofit leaders. In this section, where I set the stage for the rest of the book, I frame the history of the evaluation field and how it came to be misaligned with the nonprofits it serves. I then summarize the core mindset shifts necessary for evaluation to live up to its potential as a learning tool. By the end of this section, you'll see how evaluation could look different than it does today, and you'll be ready to jump into Parts Two and Three to make that model a reality.

Chapter One

Why Evaluation Needs a Reboot

In this chapter, I paint a picture of why evaluation needs to be reframed. Evaluation is fundamentally misaligned with the nonprofits it tries to serve. And this misalignment did not emerge out of nowhere. I share an overview of the history of evaluation and how improvement efforts of the evaluation field have increased the distance between evaluators and nonprofit leaders.

Evaluation cannot exist without nonprofits and programs, and yet evaluation has diverged from the needs of its nonprofit partners to the point of irrelevance.

Historically, evaluators and nonprofit leaders have not been close friends. Nonprofit staff work really hard to serve others, and they aren't thrilled when the evaluator walks in the door and tells them they have to work even harder to not only implement programs but also to collect data on those programs. So the nonprofit staff collect the requested data, and the evaluator comes back and tells them they aren't doing a very good job. The evaluator somehow measures a "good job" differently than the staff do. Instead of looking at environmental activism after the trail building, the evaluator looks at miles of trails built. As a result, because of a bad isolated experience or a vague feeling that evaluation won't help, many nonprofits opt out of evaluation. So, when funders ask nonprofit staff to measure impact, they scrape together some numbers to placate them.

Today's nonprofit professionals rarely experience the true power of evaluation as a tool to help them improve how they do their work. They view evaluation as busy work and something above and beyond their core jobs. But evaluation done well is central to nonprofit work and provides the assurance that you're not working hard, you're working smart. How did evaluation in practice get so far removed from its benefit to nonprofits in theory?

There isn't a singular event that separates evaluation from the nonprofits it seeks to serve. Rather, six related factors converged over time. We need to understand these factors, so we can start to see them in the evaluation work around us, and together counteract their impact:

◆ Negative perceptions of evaluation emerge through its ties with government accountability efforts.

◆ Evaluator behavior leans toward an auditor role.

◆ Evaluators develop jargon that creates a language barrier between evaluators and the nonprofits they serve.

◆ Dual goals of producing accessible and rigorous evaluation are inherently at odds.

◆ Conflict between accessibility and rigor is reinforced in evaluator training.

◆ And the same conflict between accessibility and rigor is perpetuated in evaluation practice.

Negative Perceptions

To understand evaluation's current mispositioning, we have to return to its origins to uncover its birth as a means of government accountability. This is a very abbreviated history of evaluation, just enough to provide context. There are excellent historical accounts of evaluation published elsewhere, like Stufflebeam and Shinkfield's *Evaluation Theory, Models, and Applications*[1] or Shadish, Cook, and Leviton. *Foundations of Program Evaluation.*[2]

Program evaluation, as we think of it today, has been around in the United States since at least the 1930s, when Ralph Tyler led an eight-year study of curriculum and instruction in secondary schools. Evaluation rose to prominence during the proliferation of Great Society programs in the 1960s

---

1 Stufflebeam, Daniel L., and Anthony J. Shinkfield. Evaluation Theory, Models, and Applications. San Francisco, CA: Jossey-Bass,, 2007.

2 Cook, Thomas D., Laura C. Leviton, and William R. Shadish. Foundations of Program Evaluation: Theories of Practice. Newbury Park: Sage Publications, 1991.

and 1970s. During these decades, evaluation was mandated in most federally funded programs out of fear that the multitudes of social programs were not reducing social ills. Evaluation came of age in this context, not to help programs improve, but as an accountability tool for the federal government. Early evaluators were social psychologists eager to apply methodological expertise in an applied context. These academics started discussions about the "right way" to approach evaluation that persists today.

> ### Florence Price Dwyer
>
> *It is becoming increasingly clear that much of our investment in areas [such] as education, health, poverty, and the like is not returning adequate dividends in terms of results.... One of Congress' major challenges must be to reassess our multitude of social programs, concentrate resources on programs that work where the needs are greatest, and reduce or eliminate the remainder.*
>
> **Florence Price Dwyer**
> Remarks from the US House of Representatives floor, 1970.

Evaluation has waxed and waned in popularity since the 1970s. It largely disappeared in the Reagan era, when across-the-board budget cuts dramatically reduced evaluation funding, staffing, and activities. Evaluation reemerged during Clinton's administration as government funding rebounded and, yet again, became a core mechanism of accountability in education during the 2000s. Evaluation found selective use across social programs to determine effectiveness during the Obama administration. For the first time, a movement within evaluation promoted learning instead of accountability, most notably via the "Utilization-Focused Evaluation" approach coined by Michael Quinn Patton.

> ### Former President Barack Obama on Social Services
>
> *The question we ask today is not whether our government is too big or too small, but whether it works, whether it helps families find jobs at a decent wage, care they can afford, a retirement that is dignified. Where the answer is yes, we intend to move forward. Where the answer is no, programs will end.*
>
> **Former President Barack Obama**
> Remarks at Inaugural Address, Washington, DC, January 20, 2009.

Patton's approach represents one step forward in a context of many steps back for evaluation's reputation. Only time will tell if evaluation's fluctuating prominence will continue as administrations continue to change. More recently, philanthropy has raised and further stabilized evaluation's profile since the early 2000s. While much evaluation remains driven and funded by governmental entities, foundations now dictate a portion of the work and thus the evaluation field may fluctuate less with presidential changes than during previous periods.

Through these ups and downs in popularity, evaluation has never "stuck" with social programs themselves. Evaluation remains on the periphery; an afterthought or a tool for foundations and governments to "check" on nonprofits' work. It has never become infused into the core expectations of nonprofit and social program work. And this origin of evaluation as a tool of government and funders is in and of itself problematic. It sets the expectation that evaluation should be conducted by a third party. Evaluation can never become a tool for strategic learning and improvement if it is driven by the needs of external entities, especially those occupying a position of power above nonprofits.

Evaluator Behavior

The history of evaluation as an accountability tool for governments and foundations has informed how evaluators relate to nonprofits. Many evaluators still approach nonprofits as if they are doing something wrong that needs to be identified and corrected. Much of evaluation is framed as a tool to see if nonprofits are doing what they say they are doing. This accountability focus is entirely counterproductive. It creates a fear-based relationship between client and evaluator that never ends well. The evaluator comes in and tells the nonprofit what success looks like and how to measure it.

For nonprofits, there is no potential upside: without evaluation, they can continue doing their work because "we know it works," and they can convince others it works through glowing testimonials, thus continuing the perception that evaluation is above and beyond the core work of the nonprofit. Engage in evaluation and the "expert" evaluator judges them without understanding the context in which they work and "knows better" than the nonprofit staff. Moreover, the staff can see that arrogance in the language the evaluator uses. So, the "expert" evaluator almost certainly finds out something is not working, and then the nonprofit can't go back to the status quo.

Whether actively or passively, the nonprofit resists evaluation. Remember, nonprofits are just groups of individuals, so even if the leadership is 100 percent supportive, some individuals in the nonprofit are not. They don't participate in planning or assist in data collection. And this dynamic creates a vicious self-confirming cycle. Evaluators think they understand what success looks like and how to measure the nonprofit against that bar.

As a result, the staff are turned off by the way the evaluator speaks to them, so they don't bother educating the evaluator about their program and context. The evaluator is dismayed by the lack of engagement of the program staff, which confirms that the nonprofit is low-functioning. The evaluator concludes the program does not meet the bar of success, and both leave unhappy. The staff think the bar is irrelevant, and, thus, the evaluator is irrelevant. They won't ever read the evaluation report again, and they may never do an evaluation again. The evaluator puts in all this work to create something accurate and impactful, yet no one is using it. The consultant takes this experience and projects it onto the next client, starting again with a preconceived notion of success and the unconscious assumption that nonprofits are low-functioning.

Evaluators' Jargon

Since the practice of evaluation has developed with mixed results and misunderstandings between client and consultant, the field has sought professionalization and carving out a unique practice area. Unfortunately, our approach to differentiating evaluation by developing jargon and technical language has simultaneously made it clear who is part of the "evaluation tribe" and excluded nonprofits from the conversation. We've created a language barrier between evaluators and the nonprofits we seek to serve. We spend our time redefining existing English words rather than using that energy to establish and live up to our value proposition for nonprofits.

We take a simple concept and trade the five-cent words for twenty-five-cent words with no added value. The word *evaluation* itself is a great example. Evaluators can't even agree on what evaluation means. Here is a selection of the different ways that evaluators talk about evaluation compared to the simplicity of the English definition.

Evaluation as defined by evaluators	Evaluation as defined in English
The evaluation process normally involves some identification of relevant standards of merit, worth, or value; some investigation of the performance of evaluands (that which is under study) on these standards; and some integration or synthesis of the results to achieve an overall evaluation or set of associated evaluations. —Michael Scriven	
An evaluation is examining and weighing a phenomenon (a person, a thing, an idea) against some explicit or implicit yardstick …as a means of contributing to the improvement of the program or policy. —Carol Weiss	The making of a judgment about the amount, number, or value of something.
Evaluation generates information for decision making, often answering the bottom-line question 'does it work?'… *Follow-up questions to this basic question, frequently asked by those evaluating are, 'Why does it work?' 'For whom does it work best?' 'Under what conditions does it work?' 'How do we make it better?' Evaluators provide program stakeholders with defensible answers to these important questions.* —Donaldson & Christie	

With such a big difference between how evaluators talk and how regular humans talk, it's no wonder so much of our conversation about evaluation gets stuck on, "Well, what is it?" This trend repeats again and again in evaluation, with evaluators taking words that mean something in English and giving them new definitions to better suit our needs. This pattern increases the difference between the "expert" evaluators and "novice" nonprofits.

	In Evaluation	In English
Impact	Changes that can be attributed to a particular intervention, both the intended ones and, ideally, the unintended ones.	Having a strong effect on someone or something.
Outcomes	Specific changes in attitudes, behaviors, knowledge, skills, status, or level of functioning expected to result from program activities.	The way a thing turns out; a consequence.
Output	Activities, services, events, and products that reach people who participate or who are targeted.	The amount of something produced by a person, machine, or industry.
Objective	Describes the changes you want to see, what your programs do, and answers for whom, by what degree, by when, and how it is measured.	A thing aimed at or sought; a goal.

Morever, what makes this problem so pernicious is that we focus our education in evaluation around making sure people use our new words right. How many evaluation trainings have you attended that provide a list of definitions alongside the content? Instead of focusing on the benefits of evaluation, and how to make them come to fruition, we spend our time creating new definitions and beating people over the head with them until they give up or give in.

Two Goals At Odds

Another element of evaluation professionalization has been defining standards of quality work. The four Program Evaluation Standards[3] are:

◆ **Utility:** The evaluation meets the information needs of the users.

◆ **Feasibility:** The evaluation is realistic and doable.

◆ **Propriety:** The evaluation is legal and ethical.

◆ **Accuracy:** The evaluation conveys technically adequate information.

3 Yarbrough, Donald B. *The Program Evaluation Standards: A Guide for Evaluators and Evaluation Users.* Los Angeles: Sage, 2011.

There are inherent tensions built into these four standards, and the way those tensions are managed by evaluators puts further strain on nonprofits' perception of evaluation. For example, the most accurate estimate of program impact might come from an experimental design where potential participants are randomly assigned to receive services or not. Yet to the program, this approach feels ethically suspect, violating the propriety standard by denying services to potential participants who need them. Everything in the real world is a set of trade-offs, and without clarity about who gets to decide which trade-off to make, the choice defaults to the evaluation "experts." Often nonprofits are not even aware that a trade-off has been made until the evaluation concludes. In practice, this means that the priorities of the evaluator takes precedence over the priorities of the nonprofit. Doesn't the logic seem backward given that evaluation is in service of nonprofits? Let's answer in the next section with a discussion about two competing goals.

Conflict Between Accessibility and Rigor

Yes, it is backward, but our training as evaluators—including formal education, informal on-the-job training, and continuing education at conferences—focuses inordinately on accuracy. With accuracy pounded into our heads again and again and again, evaluators' default will always be to accuracy first. I work extremely hard to balance the four standards and remind my team daily to do the same. And I have to because my evaluation upbringing was characteristic of the field's focus on accuracy.

Is Accuracy King? Sure, But...

During my doctoral studies at one of the leading evaluation training programs, my coursework included fourteen courses focused on the accuracy standard. These courses covered a broad array of evaluation and research methods so I would leave the program knowing how to generate technically accurate data. In contrast, I had only seven classes covering, at least in part, the other three standards. I agree that accuracy is important, *but it is not six times more important than utility, feasibility, and propriety.*

Accuracy is harder to teach, you say? But the messaging we get in our informal, on-the-job training is no more balanced. Consider job descriptions for evaluator positions, or even RFPs for evaluation contractors. Notice the balance of the four standards there: without exception, there is more emphasis placed on generating accurate data through rigorous methods than any of the other standards. Nor is our continuing education at conferences and events more balanced. I have found there to be more sessions on the three remaining standards in these venues than in formal and on-the-job sources, but the sessions where I see the highest engagement remain the methodological topics focused on accuracy.

Rigor Over Accessibility Is Perpetuated in Evaluation Practice

Working evaluators carry this bias toward accuracy into their work with clients. And that's where all of the elements we've discussed create a disaster. Picture an evaluator walking into a room with potential nonprofit clients. For the evaluator, the way to demonstrate qualifications is to emphasize an ability to generate methodologically rigorous, technically accurate data. The evaluator does so by chatting on and on about methods and approaches. The nonprofit staff's eyes glaze over as they think, "Well, if it were accurate but not useful to me, why would I pay for this?" It is not that accuracy is not important to nonprofits—of course, it is—but utility, including their ability to understand the evaluation, is equally important. For nonprofits, the evaluation's ability to inform their work and help them do their jobs better is the value proposition. And yet, that is rarely what evaluators emphasize. So, both parties end the meeting in frustration. The evaluator thinks, "Why don't nonprofits understand how valuable data is?" And the nonprofit staff think, "Why can't evaluators produce valuable insights for me?"

Spin-offs: Friend or Foe?

There has been a proliferation of similar but somehow different fields moving into the evaluation market—disciplines such as data science and social impact measurement.

Nonprofits are excited about these new fields. On the other hand, evaluators are annoyed because we already do this, and scared because this is our turf. In response, evaluators are spending more and more time trying to define the differences between evaluation and these other fields, *but do so from the perspective of an evaluator,* focused again on accuracy and methodology and what makes their approach different from data science and social-impact measurement. Instead of educating our new colleagues about evaluation and welcoming them into the tent, we alienate them alongside the nonprofits we hope to serve. If one of these emerging fields figures out before we do how to frame the value to social programs in a way nonprofits can understand, the evaluation field's days are numbered.

What a way to work! In an industry that is fundamentally a service industry, we've alienated the very people we claim to serve over and over again. We've done so through a persistent mismatch between our priorities and theirs, talking down to them with made-up jargon, and positioning ourselves as the ultimate judge and jury of nonprofit success. It's a wonder that evaluation hasn't talked itself out of business. If we don't start to position evaluation in a way that resonates more directly with the programs we serve, evaluation will become defunct. We're already seeing the signs of this progression during a time when social programs are deeply needed. Let me give you an example:

A Missed Opportunity

You may recall when Starbucks was in crisis after a manager kicked two black men out of a store while they were waiting for a meeting. As a result of this incident, Starbucks closed all of its stores for an

What's that? Is that a plea for program #evaluation? If only there were professionals able to help. Seriously Starbucks, washingtonpost.com has a point. Meet @aeaweb @MIEvalTIG @CES_SCE
https://lnkd.in/dzgseqZ

Perspective | Starbucks won't have any idea whether its diversity trai...
washingtonpost.com

4 Likes

Like   Comment   Share

afternoon to conduct a racial-bias training. The media wrote about how Starbucks' challenge was knowing if the racial bias training made a difference...exactly the role for evaluation. But, instead of engaging productively in the public conversation, evaluators screamed to *each other* on social media. In one of the most public conversations about program effectiveness I can remember, evaluators were irrelevant in the broader discussion. This was a prime opportunity for evaluators to connect with the people and nonprofits we purport to serve. Think about the difference it might have made if evaluators reached beyond their community. Instead of talking to one another, we could have used media, outreach, and connections to share our expertise and moved the conversation forward.

There are pockets of the evaluation field that are making progress with opportunities like this one and in the sidebar issues I've highlighted, but as a field we leave our heads in the sand. And if we continue to

Old Methods for New Causes

Among social programs, there is an increased focus on equity and social justice. For evaluation to be useful to social programs, it must match the philosophical orientation of the program. What does evaluation that promotes equity and social justice look like? I don't know yet, but I know that it does not look like forcing methodological rigor as defined decades ago by cis, white male academics, onto programs developed in service of diverse communities. And if that's the approach we continue to take, then it will no longer be an issue of nonprofits *not understanding* evaluation's value, it will be an issue of evaluation *not having* value.

do so, if we continue to frame evaluation in terms of accuracy instead of usability, use words others don't understand, and talk in terms of judgment and accountability, the evaluation field will not exist in fifty years. The field needs a reboot. It *needs to figure out its value* to the people and nonprofits it serves. The collective profession *needs to communicate* in a language that people and nonprofits understand, not in a language that professional evaluators understand. And the field *needs to shift and adapt* as the world around the field evolves. In the next chapter I share my thoughts, learned from working more than a decade in this field, about a value-proposition for evaluation that resonates with the nonprofits and social programs. Then, in the remainder of the book, I illustrate what evaluation looks like when practiced in line with that value proposition.

Chapter Two

Shifting Our Mindset

In this chapter, I share three core mindset shifts that lay the foundation for this rest of this book. These transitions are necessary to take us from the evaluation world we saw in **Chapter One** to a world where evaluation is authentically in service of nonprofits and aligned with them to improve our communities. The three mindset shifts are: finding common ground in the concepts, not the jargon; orienting toward learning and letting go of accountability; and increasing our focus on usability and accessibility as equal partners of accuracy and rigor.

Nonprofits and social programs emerge out of the best of intentions. They open their doors to help our communities and improve our world. Perhaps administrators or parents are concerned about the quality of education and declining academic achievement rates, so they start a tutoring program in low-income schools. Or a group of community leaders are troubled by food insecurity, so they establish a food bank. Or a few environmentalists are passionate about nature, so they launch a trail building program. Everyone who works in the nonprofit space does so to try to make a difference, but how do you know if your work is actually helping?

That's where evaluation comes in. In theory, evaluation provides nonprofit leaders with the information they need about what's working and what's not, so that they can improve their programs and increase their impact over time. And as evaluation helps social program staff improve their services, it helps them increase their impact, motivate funders and donors, and monitor the extent to which they are achieving their mission.

But as we learned in the previous chapter, the promise of evaluation in theory is very different than the reality of evaluation in practice. I dream of

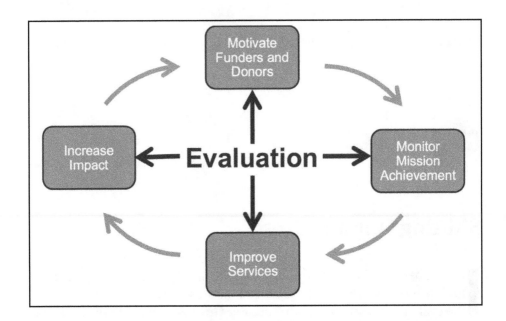

a world where evaluation and social programs are inextricably linked and best friends. In that world, everyone who touches nonprofit work, from the frontline staff to the board and donors, has an understanding of how evaluation supports social programs. Everyone has a common language to discuss evaluation design and findings in a nonpunitive, improvement-oriented context. And all evaluation is designed and conducted with that same lens of learning and improving. In that world, evaluation is perceived as a fundamental tool for improving our communities. Evaluation is infused into the day-to-day work of nonprofits. And the evaluator is a trusted thought partner and the first call when the program team comes up with a new programming idea.

This book is dedicated to strategies that help us move toward this world. But for any of the strategies in the rest of the book to succeed, we, as nonprofit professionals and evaluators, must change the way we think about this work.

Finding Common Ground in Concepts

The very first reset we need is to emphasize the questions that evaluation can answer above the methods and technical definitions that it requires. Evaluation works well when it focuses on things that people care about, uses methods that are tailored to those questions, and talks about it all in a way that everyone can understand. Without that last component, talking about evaluation in a way that everyone can understand, the best evaluations in the world mean nothing. So, let's stop arguing about the exact words that people use and find common ground in the concepts. You want to talk about social impact measurement instead of evaluation? Go for it. You don't care about the difference between outputs and outcomes and just want to focus on the most important changes in your community? Absolutely.

At its core, evaluation is about understanding what works and what doesn't so we can improve social programs and have a bigger impact on our communities. Whatever language resonates with your nonprofit to get that done, use it. But please make sure that everyone has a shared understanding and a shared language first. Everyone in the nonprofit space has evaluation baggage, so don't assume that everyone on your team is ready to find commonality in the concepts. That output and outcome distinction might be well ingrained, so use the rest of this book together to make the culture shift together and slowly. Now that we've discussed shared language, let's turn our attention to a departure from accountability and a focus on learning.

> ## Shift Together Slowly
>
> Everyone has evaluation baggage, so it might take some time to get everyone on the same terminology page. I worked with the board of directors of a new health foundation, which I describe in more detail in **Chapter Thirteen.** An important preliminary step was reorienting the team around evaluation concepts and leaving behind the definitions that each of them had picked up over the years. It took five sessions and a little over a year until it felt like we had turned the corner. Remember to stay patient and stick with it.

Orienting Toward Learning

Evaluation's roots as a tool for government accountability is one of the most pernicious and embedded challenges we have to overcome. Even the most learning-oriented evaluators I know occasionally slip into language about accountability and judgment. And despite 90 percent of the evaluation conversation being focused on learning, 10 percent hits a nerve with nonprofit staff. It throws them right back into bad memories with evaluation and sets back the process.

Evaluators cannot both be thought partners *and* judges. No one wants to share the truth of successes and failures with someone charged with grading the work. It is one or the other. And even if you think that the role of judge is still necessary, we've learned from decades of trying to make accountability-based evaluation stick that it's not what nonprofits need or want. Because evaluation doesn't exist without the engagement of nonprofits and social programs, we have to start listening to them. My team and I have addressed this challenge by working with the programs on the final "judgment." We see our roles as designing and executing the evaluation and then speaking for the data in conversations about what's next, but it's those conversations with program staff that generate the "judgment" and action plans, not us. Learn more in **Chapter Seven.**

Evaluation is powerful to the programs we serve when it adds value to the work. That should be the focus of how we talk about evaluation. I am not suggesting that evaluators falsify results to make nonprofits feel good about their work. Just as an accountability lens is not in service, neither is an undeserved pat on the back.

For evaluation to gain traction in the nonprofit space, the field has to sing one tune about the value of evaluation to help nonprofits learn about and improve programs. Then we have to deliver on that promise every time. I spend the majority of my time having conversations with nonprofit professionals about evaluation. And when they hear examples of how evaluation can inform strategic learning and ongoing improvements, their faces light up. There are examples distributed throughout this book of nonprofits that have experienced that kind of evaluation. The faster we can shift from the old governmental accountability version of evaluation to the value of nonprofits learning version of evaluation, both in words and in action, the more likely evaluation is to stick around.

Increasing Our Focus on Usability and Accessibility

Which leads us into the next major mindset shift. Evaluators and nonprofits must move beyond the heavy focus on accuracy and rigor to balance usability and accessibility. I'll say it again: even the best evaluations are worthless if the programs charged with using them don't understand them. Further, the evaluation must be aligned with the things that nonprofits want to know, even if those things don't lend themselves to traditionally rigorous methods.

For example, my colleagues and I worked with a nonprofit that knew something positive was going on but had no idea what it was. If we had been a group of researchers, we would have come up with a theory based on the literature about what was happening. Then we would have created an experimental or quasi-experimental research design using validated instruments for each potential impact area. And we may or may not have landed on the secret sauce. That's the main difference between a research approach and an evaluation approach: research will sacrifice the alignment of the answer with the question for the rigor of the design; evaluation will make the opposite decision, using a less rigorous design to answer the exact question.

So, we talked to the program staff about what they needed to understand to do their jobs better. They told us they needed to understand why kids keep coming back to the program. We focused all our evaluation resources on just that topic, using some best practices in qualitative research, but also some more undeveloped approaches. And at the end of the day, the program got what it needed. Staff gained a deep understanding of what the kids saw as the secret sauce of the program—and no one complained that the methods were not rigorous because we did not use quantitative data. Everyone was too busy incorporating well-informed changes into programs.

The combination of these three things transforms nonprofits: *concepts instead of definitions, learning instead of accountability, and focus on usability.* Nonprofits become not data-driven, but learning-driven, constantly striving to do a little better than the year before and able to access the information to inform ongoing programming tweaks through meaningful evaluation. Nonprofits see past the data and numbers to the people behind them. And they use evaluation as one more tool in their toolbox to make a difference in our communities.

Part Two

Breaking It Down: The Core Elements of Effective Evaluation

Evaluation might be on a nonprofit's radar for years before the ball ever gets rolling. For many, the cause of the delay is not knowing where to start. In this section, we break down the five core elements of effective evaluation one by one: from evaluation planning to learning from findings. By the end of the section, you have a better understanding of how to get started with evaluation and how each step can get you closer to effectively understanding how to measure your outcomes.

At its core, evaluation has five steps, the first three of which are dedicated to evaluation planning:

> *Planning*
> (1) **Mapping your program:** What exactly are you evaluating?
> (2) **Defining your key evaluation questions:** What exactly do you need to learn from an evaluation for it to be worth your time?
> (3) **Matching methods to questions:** Which evaluation methods are best suited to answer your key questions?
> (4) **Execute the evaluation:** Collect, analyze, and report on data to answer your key evaluation questions.
> (5) **Reflect and learn:** What do the evaluation findings say about your key evaluation questions? And where do you go from there?

"Matching methods to questions" and "executing the evaluation" are steps three and four and can be outsourced to an evaluation consultant or an internal evaluator. But the other three steps must be done collaboratively: you cannot outsource this thinking. The staff who touch the program daily must have a say in what is being evaluated, for what purpose, and in interpreting and learning from the evaluation. This chapter walks step-by-step through the evaluation process, highlighting key decisions and best practices.

Chapter Three

Getting Clarity So You Can Map Your Program

In this chapter, I outline the process to demonstrate clarity about exactly what you're evaluating. First, we uncover why it is important to pause and articulate what your program does and is trying to achieve even if you think you already know that. Next, we explore a step-by-step approach, refined through five years of trial and error, to help you create a program map. And last, we bridge the gap between program planning and evaluation planning with an evaluation purpose statement.

The first step of any evaluation is clearly articulating what you are evaluating. Nonprofits can evaluate what their whole nonprofit is doing, they can evaluate a particular program or a cluster of programs, or they can evaluate a particular program for a particular participant group. And making the matter more complicated, within any nonprofit, different staff looking at the program from different angles can have a very different understanding of what any given program is and is expected to do.

For example, let's look at a local after-school program that needed to develop an evaluation strategy. To begin the project, I suggested that we clarify the program that the evaluation would focus on using the approach outlined in this chapter. The program director pushed back, "We've been around since the 1990s, we already know what the program is!" I asked that she and her team humor me anyway, if for no other reason than to make sure their evaluator fully understood their program. And boy am I glad she said yes. As we completed the exercises in this chapter, it became clear that every site director had a different understanding of what the program was and what it was trying to achieve.

According to one site director, the program provided general and diverse programming to give children a safe place to go after school. Another said that the program provided only evidence-based after-school programming to promote positive youth development. These differences in perception impacted how each site planned activities, interacted with children, and spoke with external partners and funders. And these differences are often why evaluation deteriorates to the lowest common denominator of programming: number of people served. If we had designed an evaluation for any one of these perceptions, it would have made little to no sense for the other sites. But by using the process outlined in this chapter, we were able to uncover the differences and similarities across sites and strategically design an evaluation that would serve all the sites.

Program mapping is not as much an evaluation activity as it is a program planning activity, but without precise program planning, evaluation becomes a waste of resources. A clear understanding of what you are looking at is vital to evaluating and interpreting those results. This does *not* mean that programs must be simple and linear to be evaluated. Much of my work is with complex systems-level change programs. Rather, what matters is a clear articulation of what your program is trying to do, what your program does, and how those two things logically link—in other words, a program map.

Materials, Instructions, and Questions for Mapping

How do you develop a program map? In my experience, it's best done in one sitting and then tweaked slightly afterward. The first step is to make sure you have the right people in the room. Program mapping is not something you can do alone. The "must-have" staff roles include on-the-ground program staff or the people that do the work, someone from the development team or the people who secure funding for the work, and a member of the leadership team or the people who decide if the work continues.

Additional "nice-to-have" roles include a member of the communications team, a board member, or perhaps a program beneficiary. Next, carve out time and space separate from the day-to-day activities of the program. I recommend about an hour on this process, and I'll often do both this and the process outlined in **Chapter Four** during the multihour meeting. This

Activity 3.1: Mapping Your Program

Estimated time:

Forty to sixty minutes in person, thirty minutes afterward

Attendees: Consider on-the-ground program staff, nonprofit executives, development staff, communications staff, board members, and program beneficiaries. Aim for five to ten people.

Materials:

◆ Blank flash cards

◆ Markers

◆ Sticky tack/tape

◆ A big blank wall

Facilitation instructions:

◆ Assign one person to document responses on flashcards and stick them on the wall.

◆ Use a different color marker for each question below.

◆ Pause between each step and group similar responses. For example, if the program is trying to change the world for children and teachers, group the goals into these two categories. Consider color coding or adding a heading to separate the goals that you hope for children from the goals that you hope for teachers.

◆ Type up the flash cards into an electronic representation of the program map after the session.

Facilitation questions:

1. Start with the end in mind: List the things you are trying to achieve on the far right-hand side of the wall. If the program is successful, how will the world be different? These should be your big picture end goals.

2. Now take one step back: What has to occur for the end goals you just listed to materialize? How will program beneficiaries look different immediately after interacting with your program? List these items just to the left of the original list.

---

3. Activities: Next, move to the far left-hand side of the wall and post the things that make up your program. What do staff spend the most time doing? What are the critical components of your work as your participants experience it?

4. Logical links: The last step is to link the left and right side: If you do everything on the left-hand side, will the right side naturally and logically follow? If not, what is missing? Add those things to the space in the middle.

[See chart on next page]

---

time is an opportunity to step back from the day-to-day of your job and think about the big picture of what you are doing and why.

Isn't Your Mapping Process Just a Logic Model?

Sort of. The process I just described mirrors the development of a logic model. And if your program is linear and fits well into a logic model structure, by all means use that tool. *But don't let the template bully you.* I do not use logic models because I find that nonprofits get so caught up in the difference between an output and an outcome and what goes in each column that they lose track of the purpose behind mapping their program. Somehow it becomes more about having a logic model than about understanding what the program does and why. If you feel more comfortable, or a funder is asking you for it, use a logic model or theory of change template as a starting point, and adapt it for the realities of your program.

Overall Vision: Students will become engaged citizens where they are empowered to use their artistic skills to effect positive social change

What does the program expect will happen to students? (Intended Outcomes)

- Better prepared for higher education and careers as professional artists
- Increased career satisfaction
- Increased confidence (thinking big)
- Increased comfort with risk taking
- Improved entrepreneurial skills

What does the program want students to learn? (Intended Skills)

- How to create an infrastructure to make their artistic goal come to fruition
  - Formulating and executing work plans
- What is involved in the business side of art
  - Time management
  - Budgeting
  - Building a network of professional allies
  - Marketing and communication

What do students experience through the program?

- Resume building activities
- Process of applying for funding
- Experiential / learning
- Exposure to different educational and career opportunities available to artists
- Relationships with professional artists

What are the main program components?

- **Student Grants:** Provide seed funding for the creation of new work (7-10 students per year)
- **Alumni Internship:** Brings IAA alumni back to campus as student teachers (1-2 alumni per year)
- **Strategic Partnerships:** Matches IAA students with outside arts and education organizations for volunteering and professional development opportunities (up to 7 partners per year)
- **Master Classes:** Opportunities for more engaged and interactive mentoring relationships with professional artists (6-10 classes per year)
- **Alumni Lecture Series:** IAA graduates share their experiences in higher education and the professional arts world with the current student body (6-8 lectures per year)

What programmatic and institutional factors influence the program?

- Shift in mission/goals of AEL over time, based on changing codirectors
- Shifts in budget allocation of AEL components
- Shifts in IAA student population:
  - Changes in student interest
  - Attraction of socially active students
  - More international students after 2008
- New IAA program, Arts in Society, focused on the role of artists in society

Model type:	Logic Models graphically illustrate program components, helping you clearly identify program inputs and activities and the anticipated outcomes of the work.	Theories of Change graphically illustrate a causal path linking activities and outcomes and explaining how and why the desired outcomes are plausible.
Select this framework if you:	◆ Have never visually mapped your program before. ◆ Want a clear and concise "at-a-glance" picture of what your program does. ◆ Need to clarify the basic building blocks of your program. ◆ Want to summarize a complex program into basic categories.	◆ Already have a logic model. ◆ Want an "at-a-glance" picture of why your program does what it does *and* who your program influences. ◆ Need to clarify the linkages between program components. ◆ Have complex, interconnected programming.
For additional information, I recommend:	University of Wisconsin's "Extension School Online Logic Model Course"[4]	Centre for Social Action Innovation Fund's (CSAIF) "Guidance for Developing a Theory of Change for Your Programme"[5]

Do I Map My Program or My Nonprofit?

It helps to start this mapping process before deciding on the boundaries of your map. Often the end goals you specify help determine how much of a

---

4 "Welcome to Enhancing Program Performance with Logic Models," https://lmcourse.ces. uwex.edu.

5 "Guidance for Developing a Theory of Change for Your Programme," Nesta, The Social Innovation Partnership: https://media.nesta.org.uk/documents/theory_of_change_ guidance_for_applicants_.pdf.

nonprofit's programming should be captured on the same program map. For example, how cohesive are the changes you want to see in participants? If all your programs are working toward the same end goal through the same changes, consider mapping at the nonprofit level. Look at the second step of Activity 3.1 to learn more. If not, consider a program-by-program map. I've seen this shift both ways: one nonprofit wanted to visualize the whole nonprofit, but during the program mapping process realized programs were trying to achieve such dramatically different things the map could not adequately display them all. Another nonprofit wanted to map at the program level before realizing programs were so interconnected that a nonprofit map made more sense.

Other factors to consider include how your nonprofit is funded and how your nonprofit is staffed. If most of your funding is general operating support, a nonprofit-wide map might make most sense. If, instead, you receive primarily project-based funds, each program may need its own map.

The same logic applies to staffing. If your staff primarily work on one program or another, a program-by-program map may be a good fit. If your staff work across programs, a nonprofit-wide map helps reduce complexity and confusion.

The Evaluation Purpose Statement

I bet you are thinking the process I described above sounds more like program planning than evaluation. And you're right, it is. Good program planning undergirds all good evaluation. Once you have a clear understanding of what you are evaluating, you can then begin thinking about what you want to learn. That's the focus of our next chapter.

But before we get there, I always encourage the nonprofits I work with to create an evaluation purpose statement. An evaluation purpose statement is a two-sentence summary of why you want to do evaluation in the first place and what the results will be used for. It's a bit like a mission statement, but just for your evaluation. We have gotten to the point where evaluation is such a buzzword in nonprofit and foundation work that we assume all nonprofits should be evaluating everything and for the same reasons. But that is not true. Evaluation should serve an intended purpose.

The first sentence of your purpose statement should articulate what you want to learn through evaluation. Do you want to determine whether your program is effective? And effective at what specifically? Do you want to know

Getting A Bird's-Eye View

Evaluation can be used to improve programs, to monitor progress towards a mission, or to more clearly articulate to external stakeholders what a program does and why. Each of these purposes dictate different approaches to evaluation. For instance, the former requires an evaluation more able to distinguish the specific contributions of individual program components, whereas the latter benefits from a more holistic view. Before you even get into key evaluation questions in our next chapter, it's important to sit down and think about the thirty-thousand-foot view of why you are dedicating resources to evaluation in the first place.

whether your program is being implemented appropriately? Do you want to determine whether it's reaching the right people? Solving a real problem? Making a long-term impact on the community? Changing the system? The clearer you can be at the beginning about why you're doing evaluation, the more likely you are to get, in the end, what you want out of an evaluation.

The second sentence of your evaluation purpose statement should include a clear articulation of how you're going to use the results. Are you going to actually use the results to improve your programs or are they just going to sit on a shelf? And, if you don't have the power or position to improve your program, is it worth spending resources on evaluation in the first place? Are you going to use the results to communicate with funders? Donors? Beneficiaries?

Sentence 1: What do you want to learn through an evaluation?	Sentence 2: How will you use the results?
The purpose of the evaluation is to explore what areas of Positive Youth Development Program A impact attending youth and which components of the program are the most effective.	Evaluation results will be used to advance programming to increase effectiveness and to report to funders.
The purpose of evaluation is to determine how effectively Program B builds capacity of local nonprofits to improve the quality of life for residents.	The results will be used to continually refine and improve Program B and, in turn, to effectively communicate what we do and why.
The purpose of the evaluation is to connect the dots between Program C processes and program, short-term outcomes reported by families, and long-term outcomes highlighted in the research base.	The results will be used to articulate the strengths and weaknesses of Program C and, in turn, optimize our work.
The purpose of the evaluation is to detail what Nonprofit D does and which components of our work are the most effective.	Evaluation results will be used to advance programming by ensuring Nonprofit D can clearly define activities, add value to clients and increase effectiveness by continuing to refine our programming.
The purpose of evaluation is to determine if and how Nonprofit E's content inspires viewers to engage in civic action.	The results will be used to prioritize content and position Nonprofit E as a community leader and resource.
Additional Reading: Preskill, H., & Russ-Eft, D. (2015). *Building evaluation capacity: Activities for teaching and training (Second Edition)*. Sage Publications.	

It is critical that everyone within your nonprofit, particularly those involved in resource distribution, such as your executive directors and your board members, are bought into the evaluation purpose statement. The purpose statement sets the stage for why evaluation is important and why it's worth investing financial and human capital. Purpose statements tend to convey a longer timeframe than key evaluation questions: a purpose statement captures the big-picture reasoning for five to ten years, whereas key evaluation questions might guide an evaluation for one to three years. Let's learn more about key evaluation questions now.

Chapter Four

Creating Great Questions to Guide Your Evaluation

If I could wave a magic wand and have all nonprofits implement one evaluation planning strategy, it would be key evaluation questions. Creating great questions to guide your evaluation is the most important element to effective evaluation. In this chapter, I outline the process for articulating the most important things you want to learn from an evaluation. By the end of these exercises, you have "marching orders" for your evaluation that ensure the end product teaches you something new and something you care about.

Now that you have more clarity about "my program" by completing the mapping process, the next step is to get more specific about what "to evaluate" means to you: what do you really want to know when you are at the end of this evaluation process? I recommend defining key evaluation questions to specify what aspects of a program will be evaluated based on what you want to know most.[6] Key evaluation questions help you specify why you want to do an evaluation at all and what you want to learn as a result of that evaluation. Without key evaluation questions, you're rolling the dice: if you are not clear up front about your learning expectations, you are letting whoever is implementing the evaluation make those decisions, and you may not end up with the information you need at the end of the day.

This pattern of unclear expectations leads the evaluator to make assumptions produces an end product that doesn't address what you care about. It's what makes evaluation feel useless so much of the time.

6 Lori Wingate, Evaluation Questions Checklist, Daniela Schroeter, School of Public Affairs and Administration, Western Michigan University, 2016, https://www.wmich.edu/evaluation/checklists.

For example, a local nonprofit spent ten years with an evaluator partner focused on the educational outcomes of the program. When transitioning to working with me, I walked staff through the process outlined in this chapter and found that what they really wanted to know was how well the program integrated into communities! No wonder previous evaluations felt useless! Let's break the cycle together and go into each and every evaluation with a clear and explicit statement of what the evaluation must deliver for it to be a worthwhile use of your time, money, and energy.

Besides the benefits of key evaluation questions aligning the evaluation focus with your learning priorities, key evaluation questions also strengthen evaluation reports. Instead of following a research model where you report findings by each data collection method, such as survey results first followed by focus group results, gather the findings by key evaluation question, so all the information in response to each question is together. This avoids saddling the reader with synthesizing findings between sources. The image below shows the table of contents of an evaluation report structured in this way.

Table of Contents

Understanding Different Types of Questions

Before we get into the "how-to" of key evaluation questions, I want to be clear on a very important distinction between key evaluation questions, strategy questions, and survey or interview questions. Your key evaluation questions are *not* something that you would ask directly of program beneficiaries. Rather, your key evaluation questions are the big-picture questions that you are asking of your evaluation to make it useful.

If your evaluation was sitting in this room, starting a job at your nonprofit, the key evaluation questions would be regarding roles and responsibilities. You would say, "Hey evaluation, it's your job to help me understand the extent to which our programs build early literacy skills among our beneficiaries." Or, "Hey evaluation, it is your job to help me understand the extent to which our program is being implemented with fidelity and the extent to which that fidelity leads to changes in students' reading achievement." You are not going to take your key evaluation questions and put them on a survey. You're not going to say, "Hey participant, to what extent was this program implemented with fidelity?"

Key evaluation questions are also *not* strategy questions. Strategy questions are forward-looking that ask questions about what a program *should* do. Key evaluation questions address what a program *is* doing. The two are related, but not the same: key evaluation questions identify the pieces of information you need to know to answer a strategy question. For example, if your strategy question is, "How do we increase third-grade reading proficiency?" your evaluation questions might look something like, "To what extent does program X increase early literacy skills?" and "To what extent does program Y cultivate children's love of

---

Strategy Questions: What the organization/program *should* do.

e.g., How do we increase third grade reading proficiency?

↑

Evaluation questions inform the answer to strategy questions

Evaluation Questions: What the organization/program *is doing*.

e.g., To what extent does program X increase

early literacy skills?

Evaluation questions dictate what you ask program beneficiaries

↓

Survey/Interview Questions: How an *individual beneficiary* is doing on a *sub-component* of your evaluation question.

e.g., To what extent are the children in your classroom able

to distinguish between letters, before and after program X?

reading?" Key evaluation questions live in the middle ground between strategy questions and survey or interview questions. They dictate what you are going to ask participants and feed into the strategy questions that you need to answer as a nonprofit.

Generating and Framing Key Evaluation Questions

Your key evaluation questions explicate what you need to learn from an evaluation to make it worthwhile. There are two parts to developing key evaluation questions: first, you must figure out the topics that your key evaluation questions should focus on. Then, you make sure they are written in a way that positions the evaluation for success. What do you need to learn from an evaluation so it's worth your time at the end of the day? There are three places to start looking for key evaluation question topics:

Your Brain and Your Team's Collective Intelligence

The first and most important thing about key evaluation questions is that they should feel relevant to the people who you are asking to do the legwork of the evaluation. Start with your program staff: What do they want to know about the program? What keeps them up at night? What information would help them do their jobs better? I often hear from nonprofit leaders who have tried to implement new evaluation efforts and experienced pushback from the staff. The first question I ask is, "Who developed the evaluation effort?" The answer is always, "Well I did," and that is why staff are resisting: because the value of the additional work is not directly related to them. The more that staff members who are involved in the evaluation contribute to developing the focus of the evaluation, the more they will see the value in taking the time to participate in the data collection you're asking them to do.

Your Program Map

Are there parts of your program that jump out at you as the most critical to achieving your goals and mission? Often programs have many different components and they're not all equally important. An evaluation has limited resources, and you have to make some tough decisions about what you're going to focus on. How to prioritize depends on what is most important in your program map: you won't always look at long-term end goals, which can be the most expensive to evaluate well and dependent on several intermediate successes happening first.

Activity 4.1: Creating Key Evaluation Questions
Method One — Your Brain

Estimated time: Thirty or more minutes

Attendees: Consider on-the-ground program staff, nonprofit executives, development staff, communications staff, board members, program beneficiaries. Aim for five to ten people.

Materials:

◆ Blank flash cards

◆ Markers

◆ Sticky tack tape

◆ A big blank wall

◆ Three numbered sticky dots for each person

Facilitation Instructions:

◆ Give each individual a stack of flashcards and a marker. Your role is to take completed cards and stick them to the wall in a random order.

◆ Have participants write down what they want to know most about the program. Each question should be on its own card. Participants can write as many or as few as they'd like.

◆ Ask two to three people to come up and group similar questions. Cards should only be stacked if they are exactly identical, but similar cards should be near one another. Have the volunteers explain to the room which groups they created.

◆ Give each individual a set of three dots to rank order the three questions that are most important, subjectively. Place the dot, labeled "1," on the most important question and so on.

◆ Review areas of agreement and discuss areas of dissent until you reach consensus on a set of important questions. Aim for only three to five questions.

◆ Now, you have a prioritized list of the most important questions to your program staff. Hang onto it and proceed with the other two sources.

Activity 4.2: Creating Key Evaluation Questions
Method Two — Your Program Map

Estimated time: Fifteen minutes

Attendees: Consider on-the-ground program staff, nonprofit executives, development staff, communications staff, board members, and program beneficiaries. Aim for five to ten participants.

Materials:

◆ Reproduced program map, large on a wall for all to see

◆ One sticky dot for each person

Facilitation Instructions:

◆ Give each individual a sticky dot.

◆ Have each individual review the program map and place a dot on the component or linkage that feels the most critical to the program. What would make the program fall apart if it was removed?

◆ After everyone has added dots, have each individual explain the placement.

◆ Based on these results, consider whether any additions to the list developed in Activity 3.2 make sense. Also, consult the third source discussed in Activity 4.3, compare, and settle on a final list of three to five key evaluation questions.

Imagine if you spend all your resources evaluating your long-term end goal and found your program was not successful in achieving it. Would you be able to figure out why? It's a better use of resources, especially in the first years of evaluation, to identify some intermediate steps in your program map that are critical to achieving your long-term goals. Are there any parts of the program which, if you removed one component, would fall apart? Well, you better make sure that part is working! Are there other areas of your program that get you in the door with your clients? If you can't get people in the door, you can never achieve your long-term goal. Start with a focus on those intermediate elements.

The Existing Evidence Base

Evaluation can never evaluate everything about a program. You could spend your entire program budget on evaluation and still not rigorously evaluate every detail of the program. So make the best use of your available evaluation resources by building on existing research and evaluation in similar programs. Target your evaluation dollars in areas where the least is known. Consider obesity prevention: evaluation of obesity prevention programs used to focus on measuring the body mass index (BMI) of beneficiaries before and after a program. But over the years, the academic research became clearer that the two key levers for obesity prevention were fruit and vegetable consumption and physical activity.

As a result, individual programs didn't need to re-make that connection. They did not need to re-prove that fruit and vegetable consumption and physical activity led to obesity reduction. Individual programs could focus evaluation resources on establishing that a particular intervention led to fruit and vegetable consumption and/or a physical activity increase, and then rely on the research to make that last leap to obesity prevention. In this way, obesity prevention programs take advantage of areas that already have strong research backing to make the best use of the evaluation resources they have. Look into the research for your content area and consider which areas already have a strong research backing. Compare these well-understood topics with those that are newly introduced and that the field knows less about.

How Do You Frame Key Evaluation Questions?

After you know what your key evaluation questions should be about, the trick is to frame them in a way that makes them as useful as possible. My go-to resource is the Key Evaluation Checklist, which suggests that key evaluation questions should be evaluative, pertinent, reasonable, specific, and answerable:

Evaluative

Key evaluation questions should focus on some aspect of the quality, worth, or significance of a program. "How many people did we serve?" is not an evaluative question; it is purely descriptive and provides no additional information to assess whether or not a program is worth doing. But "Do the demographics of our participants match the demographics of the school we serve?" is evaluative for a program that aims to serve the same at-risk students as the local school district.

In this case, the program's ability to access its target population is critical to its success. Similarly, "Which programs should we dedicate more resources to?" is not an evaluative question, but a strategic one. But, "Which programs are most strongly linked to improving positive youth development for

Activity 4.3: Creating Key Evaluation Questions
Method Three — The Existing Evidence Base

Estimated Time: Unlimited, start with two hours

Attendees: Solo or pair activity

Not all evidence is created equal. Some evidence is more rigorously tested than others. If every kind of evidence were on the rungs of a ladder, peer-reviewed literature would be on the top rung. Start here by using Google Scholar or a database of published journals such as JAMA, the journal of the American Medical Association. Here you'll find "scientific studies" that have been published in journals only after passing rigorous reviews by fellow researchers. Below, I've listed how you can go about conducting this kind of top-rung research. After you've completed this rung, go down to the next step and look at grey literature, and still further down to content experts.

◆ Create a list of keywords to search

   ❖ Ask yourself a couple of questions, such as:

      ❖ What problem am I trying to tackle?

      ❖ What are factors that I know lead to the problem?

      ❖ What strategies am I planning to use to tackle the problem?

      ❖ What group of people am I working with?

      ❖ What is the setting of my work?

   ❖ Find synonyms for your answers to expand your keyword list.

   ❖ Adding "Systematic review" to your search can help find articles that review multiple articles on your topic.

   ❖ Use advanced search options in the database or browser to narrow your search.

◆ Search for keywords in Google Scholar (google.com/scholar)

   ❖ Click on the arrow to the right of the search box to bring up the advanced search window that lets you search in the author, title, and publication fields, as well as limit your search results by date.

   ❖ Consider using Boolean logic in Google Scholar to boost your search.

◆ Start with an article you know relates to your area of interest

   ❖ Review its reference list for articles.

   ❖ Search databases or Google Scholar for the article's authors to learn what else they have published.

   ❖ Note the keywords listed in the article and use them in searches.

   ❖ Search for the article in Google Scholar.

      ❖ Find other articles that cited the article by clicking "Cited by…"(see arrow, below).

      ❖ Find similar articles by clicking "Related articles" (see arrow, below).

Towards program theory validation: Crowdsourcing the qualitative analysis of participant experiences

E Harman, T Azzam - **Evaluation** and program planning, 2018 - Elsevier

This exploratory study examines a novel tool for validating program theory through crowdsourced qualitative analysis. It combines a quantitative pattern matching framework traditionally used in theory-driven evaluation with crowdsourcing to analyze qualitative …

☆ 〝〞 Cited by 2   Related articles   All 6 versions

Next, search grey literature that is published by a credible entity. For instance, a foundation report; a Centers for Disease Prevention and Control study; or research commissioned by a specific group and published by that group without review by other researchers.

◆ To find grey literature, search for the same key words using:

   ❖ Google, rather than Google Scholar

   ❖ Grey Literature Report or GreyLit.org for publications from governmental entities and nonprofits

   ❖ The Clearinghouse on Assessment and Evaluation at Ericae.net

◆ Pay close attention to:

   ❖ Who published the document.

   ❖ Is it a well-known nonprofit or institute?

   ❖ What are the nonprofit's priorities? Does it have political interests that could influence the report's findings?

❖ When it was published.

❖ What sources it cites.

If neither peer-reviewed nor grey literature is available, are there content experts in your field that you can reach out to? University-based researchers often know what research is up and coming. Maybe it's been presented at a conference but not yet published. Lastly, reach out to practice experts in your field, like other nonprofits implementing similar programs. They may have internal evaluation results that speak to the same questions you are asking.

Revisit your draft key evaluation questions from the other two sources (Activities 4.1 and 4.2). Are there any questions for which the answer is already well established in the literature? If so, consider removing or revising those questions. After comparing all three sources, settle on a final list of three to five key evaluation questions. Remember, these questions are not forever; they are for now and can and should evolve as you learn from evaluation.

---

participants?" is evaluative for a positive youth development nonprofit because it measures the program's ability to improve outcomes for participants, and in turn, can inform the strategic question.

Pertinent

Somebody has to care about the answer to the key evaluation question and, ideally, the answer should inform some kind of strategic decision. If you followed the process outlined in Activity 4.1, you've guaranteed that your key evaluation questions are pertinent. I see the pertinence of key evaluation questions most at risk when the direct program staff and nonprofit leadership are not involved in developing them: outside evaluators select key evaluation questions that they think are most answerable or would be interesting to answer. Only by chance do they identify questions pertinent to the nonprofit. It's an easily preventable risk: don't outsource evaluation planning. Be actively involved in defining the focus of your evaluation regardless of who will end up executing the evaluation.

Reasonable

Key evaluation questions must represent a reasonable expectation of the program. I see problems in this area most often with short-term, drop-in interventions. "After a one-hour after-school tutoring program, our at-risk students are going to graduate from high school!" Okay, maybe they will, but it won't be because of your one hour of tutoring. The other area in which I frequently see unreasonable key evaluation questions is with programs that are deeply embedded in a web of connected interventions. In this case, the network of interventions might produce dramatic results, but it is unreasonable to expect any one element to produce those outcomes. Consider the scope of your program compared with the outcomes you seek to achieve. Understanding what past similar programs have achieved can provide a helpful reality check. See Activity 4.2.

Specific

It is not useful to frame an evaluation by saying, "We want to know if we are making a difference." Evaluation implies a focus on whether a nonprofit makes a difference, that's what evaluation is for. But as we talked about at the beginning of this section, such a broad statement of what you want to get out of evaluation does not help focus and direct the evaluation one bit. Take the necessary time to identify what kind of impact you are seeking and frame the key evaluation question more narrowly.

Answerable

Sometimes even the most important questions encounter resource and logistical barriers. Imagine you are an after-school program and you want to look at academic achievement. How feasible is the data-sharing agreement process to get academic achievement data from your school district? For some, it may be doable. For others, it's not possible. In the district where I live and work, I have never heard of a nonprofit external to the district successfully getting a data-sharing agreement in less than three years. Here, we are structurally limited in our ability to answer academic achievement questions, so we table those questions. We often leave them on our list, mark them "aspirational" and, instead, allocate our resources toward something that we can actually evaluate.

Insider Tips

Now that we've covered framing key evaluation questions, here are some insider tips I've gathered over the years about question development, and I'd love to share them with you.

How Many Questions

How many questions should I have? The Key Evaluation Checklist recommends that as a set, your list of key evaluation questions should be complete and explicate all you want to know from your evaluation. I disagree, because in my experience, programs have more unanswered questions than can be tackled in any evaluation. I find that between three and five questions are answerable during an evaluation. On the higher side, you get more surface-level information about a lot of things; on the lower side, you can get deep information about only a few things.

The Beauty of TWE

My team jokes that I need a "TWE" t-shirt because I start every single key evaluation question with, "To what extent..." No programs are ever all good or all bad. When you ask a "Does..." question, it implies a yes or no answer that does not exist. "To what extent..." allows for nuance and gray area. The more your questions account for gray area, the more you can learn about that gray area and you can work to expand the circumstance and populations for which your programs work.

Don't Fear Subquestions

Don't be afraid to use subquestions to add depth to key evaluation questions. Subquestions help you dig deeper and explore differences based on participant characteristics, program variation, and different sites of a program. They can also help you ask why certain results occur. For example, your main key evaluation might be "To what extent does program X increase early literacy skills?" and you might include a subquestion like "Do these results differ for schools with a high free and reduced lunch rate?"

Define Your Terms

Key evaluation questions should make sense to people outside your program. Remember, you will use them not only to frame your evaluation design but also to structure how you report findings. So, it's critical that anyone who might be reading your findings understands what the questions are asking and why they matter. Your whole nonprofit might know what your program acronym means, but external people should also be able to look at your key evaluation questions and recognize the value of knowing the answer without you there to explain it.

The same logic applies for program names: at my company, we have a program called "single touchpoint trainings," but we recognize that means something more specific to us than to external stakeholders, so we only use this language internally. Branded program names are ubiquitous in nonprofit work but not always a useful way to represent programs. Try to take out the jargon and the specific programming language and, instead, speak in plain English for your key evaluation questions.

Sample Key Evaluation Questions	Program Type
To what extent does our content drive audience members to take civic action? What types of content are most effective? Which audiences take civic action? Which don't?	An established and stable public television channel with new aspirations to influence the civic dialogue.
To what extent does participating in Program A contribute to the development of early literacy skills?	An established volunteer-led supplemental literacy program in public preschool classrooms.
To what extent is Program B implemented with fidelity? What factors support or impede successful implementation?	An old but recently changed supplemental literacy program in public elementary school classrooms.
To what extent do participating centers increase their oral health promotion practices? To what extent are these practices sustainable?	A pilot program to teach early childcare centers how to promote positive oral health.
To what extent are partners, clients, and communities better off after applying the Knowledge, Skills, and Abilities (KSA) taught by Nonprofit C to increase their capacity and support to collaborate? Toward what end are clients applying KSA's from Nonprofit C?	A new program at an established nonprofit to support collaborative efforts and spread collaboration best practices.

To what extent does Program D create a safe space for individuals experiencing homelessness or poverty to connect with our nonprofit, each other, and the community?	A pilot program for populations experiencing homelessness at a local library.
To what extent is the training curriculum aligned with job descriptions and demands? As perceived by: ◆ The health center managers ◆ The health center assistants ◆ The regional directors	A training program for non-licensed medical staff, anticipating a major revision of the program structure and content.
In what ways is Nonprofit E building capacity among local nonprofits? In what ways are we not?	A maturing community foundation more focused on capacity building than grant dollar distribution.
How and to what extent have Nonprofit F's actions directly or indirectly impacted primary care in the state?	A large health foundation looking back at a decade of funding in a particular area.

Chapter Five

Choosing the Right Methods to Answer Your Questions

By now, your mapping process and key evaluation questions have put you in a good frame of mind to ponder research methods. We've finally arrived at the decisions that more closely resemble what comes to mind when you think of evaluation: figuring out which methods and data sources to use. Nonprofit staff often tell me they want to do a survey. In the days of easily accessible and free online survey platforms, surveys have become ubiquitous in nonprofit work. But surveys are not always the right method to help you answer your key evaluation questions.

In this chapter, we take a closer look at which evaluation approaches are best for different types of key evaluation questions. We talk through the differences between quantitative and qualitative data and the advantages of using both. And we end the chapter with some tips on how to know which data sources are best for your key evaluation questions. Even if you never plan on conducting an evaluation yourself, it's important to understand when each data source makes the most sense, so you can be an informed consumer of evaluation information and a support system for those within your nonprofit who are conducting evaluation.

Scale and Scope Versus How and Why

A common dichotomy in research methods is the qualitative-quantitative distinction. This split is useful for thinking about which broad categories of methods might fit best. But it's had a terribly negative side effect of introducing a false hierarchy, where quantitative data is perceived as superior to qualitative data. And as a result of this perception, well-done qualitative data is dramatically underused in program evaluation. It's a shame because nonprofits are fundamentally about people, and qualitative data is what helps the stories come alive in evaluation.

So, let me clear this up right away: quantitative data is *not* inherently "better" or "more rigorous" than qualitative data. Both quantitative data and qualitative data can be high-quality and rigorous when used to answer key evaluation questions they are well suited for, and when executed according to best practices for that method. But when a collection method is used to answer a poorly suited key evaluation question or when it is executed poorly, that evaluation is going to be poor quality *regardless* of whether it is qualitative or quantitative. For example, using quantitative data to answer a question that asks about the lived experience of participants is a mismatch.

The easiest way to think about the difference between quantitative data and qualitative data is that quantitative data captures the *scale and scope,* while qualitative data captures the *how and why*. If you are primarily interested in understanding how much knowledge participants are gaining in terms of *scope*, or how many participants are gaining knowledge with regard to *scale*, quantitative data is the way to go. If you are, instead, interested in *how* participants are learning and what they are doing with that knowledge afterward to determine the *why*, qualitative data is a better fit. In an ideal world, we learn both halves of that puzzle: how much knowledge are participants gaining *and* what are they doing with that knowledge. As evaluators, we talk about the magic in the mix—that is, we

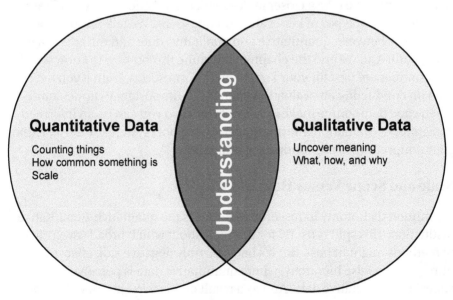

learn the most when we combine sources of quantitative data with sources of qualitative data.

Within the broad distinction of "scale and scope" and "how and why," quantitative and qualitative data have different strengths:

Quantitative Data	Qualitative Data
Scale & Scope	*How & Why*
Precise, specific, concrete	Explore a topic you know little about
Test existing theories	Capture the "lived experience" of your beneficiaries
Capture or predict cause and effect relationships	Give voice to the "how" and "why" of your quantitative results
Generalize and replicate findings	Explore an emotionally sensitive topic
	Explore issues with a difficult-to-access group

Quantitative Data

Let's take a closer look at the circumstances in which pursuing quantitative data can be useful and what some of those scenarios might look like.

Precise, Specific, or Concrete Data

You might have a funder who asks, "How many people did you serve? Or how many people gained knowledge as a result of participating in your program?" These questions tend to be concrete proxies for more complex, nuanced statements of what the program is actually trying to do. For example, there might be several topics about which you are trying to build knowledge. They require a level of precision not possible with qualitative data and do not call for the rich detail that qualitative data provide; thus, they dictate a quantitative approach.

Test Existing Theories

Quantitative data is best when you already have a strong understanding of what is going on and you want to confirm or disconfirm that working theory. This is the most common reason I recommend quantitative data to programs: when you have a working theory based on years of evaluation or direct experience with the program, and you want to understand whether it's happening consistently across beneficiaries.

Predicting Cause and Effect Relationships

When your program has matured to the point where you need to unequivocally demonstrate that your program *caused* a change in your participants, you need quantitative data. Specifically, quantitative data with an experimental or quasi-experimental design is necessary when you need to demonstrate that participants saw positive changes *because* they participated in your program, and only because they participated in your program. Programs only hit this level of readiness when their models are stable and implemented consistently, and when they have early data showing that positive changes are occurring to which they contribute. By the way, fewer than one in fifty of the programs I interact with are ready for this type of evaluation.

Generalize and Replicate Findings

Quantitative data is always going to be better at helping you understand when something is happening across a large number of participants because it can generalize across a population. Unlike qualitative data, when working with quantitative data you attempt to ensure that the group of people responding to you matches the key demographic characteristics of the entire universe of people you serve. In research-speak, we say that your sample is "representative of your population."

Qualitative Data

Now that we've explored scenarios where scale and scope are the priority, let's examine the pursuit of qualitative data, or answering the "how and why" questions.

Explore a Topic You Know Little About

We talked earlier about quantitative data helping you test theories. Qualitative data helps you build those theories. When you don't have a strong understanding of what your participants are experiencing and what benefits your program is producing, prioritize qualitative data. You might hear qualitative evaluations termed "exploratory," because they excel at helping you explore perspectives and experiences.

Rich, Lived Experience

Qualitative data is great at capturing the details and story of your beneficiaries' experience. If you want to understand not just whether your theory holds, but why your theory is working or not working, qualitative data can help you understand what is happening with your participants as they experience your program.

Voice to the How and Why of Quantitative Data

Say you've committed to a fully quantitative evaluation. You get the data back, and you're not seeing the results you hoped for. Your participants are not gaining the knowledge, skills, and abilities that you were hoping for. Why not? The quantitative data alone can't answer why. That's where qualitative data shines: digging deeper and understanding the how and why behind a result that you're seeing in the numbers.

Explore an Emotionally Sensitive Topic

When you are asking people about something emotionally sensitive, such as immigration experiences, domestic violence, and homelessness, qualitative data is always preferred. Why? Because quantitative data collection can feel cold and impersonal. As staff members in a social program, you spend years building positive supportive relationships with your participants. Evaluation is an extension of that relationship, and when you ask about personal topics impersonally, you can do major damage to those relationships. A good rule of thumb is, if you wouldn't want to share something with the black box of the Internet, don't ask your participants to. Instead, use in-person qualitative methods like interviews.

Access Hard to Reach Populations

When using quantitative data, you need to know all of the people who you're collecting data from in advance, and you need to have some way to contact them, whether that's an email address, a physical address, or a phone number. With qualitative data, you don't have to know that information up front. Qualitative data can be helpful when you don't know or have access to the group you're trying to learn about.

Mixing Methods

The strengths and weakness of quantitative and qualitative data highlight areas where mixing the data is most helpful. For example, you might use qualitative data to build a theory of what is happening and apply quantitative data to test it. This first example in research speak is "sequential mixed methods": using one method first to inform how you use the second. Another approach is called "concurrent mixed methods," which uses two different methods at the same time to capture different angles on the same thing. For example, you might use quantitative data to build a concrete, precise summary of your program, while using qualitative data to illuminate the stories and experiences behind that data. To help you determine your mix of methods, let's explore the importance of context:

Practical Strengths of Qualitative Data

Let's say you're working with homeless populations. It might be challenging to get a list of all of the people you want to collect data from at the beginning, unless they participated in a very specific program. Because the way you collect data is different with qualitative data, you can use something called "snowball sampling," which means that you start with the people that you know and then use them to find additional people. You might start with five people who you know are experiencing homelessness and ask them, "Do you know anyone else that I should be talking to that had a similar or a different experience than you did?" In this way, qualitative data has a practical strength when you're exploring issues with a difficult to access group.

Looking at Methods in the Context of Your Questions

Now that we've talked about the strengths and weaknesses of both data types, let's come back to which key evaluation questions are better for one type, the other, or both. In the section about key evaluation questions, I pushed for specificity in questions—the idea that you shouldn't just say, "I want to evaluate the impact of my programs." This is where that becomes critically important. If you simply say, "the impact of my programs," then it is not at all clear whether quantitative or qualitative data is the best fit. But let's compare two programs: the first is an early-literacy program providing supplemental reading volunteers to Head Start Programs. Staff decided on the key evaluation question, "To what extent does the program increase pre-literacy skills among participating three- to five-year-olds?" This question is a great fit for quantitative data because:

◆ Preliteracy skills are a well-established concept, where the research base has developed a strong understanding of what preliteracy skills for three- to five-year-olds includes. The data is precise and concrete.

◆ The academic research has a strong understanding of how those preliteracy skills develop, and the program was designed in alignment with that theory. The data is based on an existing theory.

◆ The program varies little between the enrolled early childcare classrooms and is consistently delivered throughout the school year. The data is generalizable.

Now compare that example to the program I introduced in **Chapter Three:** a drop-in after-school program where staff members within the program each have a slightly different understanding of what the program does and is trying to achieve. The key evaluation question they selected was "From an exploratory lens, what types of impacts are participants experiencing, and what components of our programs are most linked to those impacts?" This question is a great fit for qualitative data:

◆ There is no existing program theory and, in fact, the staff are unclear what is happening in their program. The data explores a new topic.

◆ The staff expressed an interest in understanding the program from the lens of the participants, instead of the staff. The data captures "lived experiences."

◆ The drop-in nature of the program combined with spotty attendance records makes data collection across all participants challenging. The data is hard to access.

But remember, true understanding of your key evaluation questions comes from the intersection of qualitative and quantitative data. In both of these examples, one data type played the lead role, but the other data type was included in a supporting capacity. In the literacy program, rich qualitative data was also captured through focus groups comprised of teachers to enhance their understanding of the role the program played in preliteracy skills. In the after-school program, attendance records were also enhanced to understand which sites and activities generated the highest return attendance.

Types of Data Sources

There is an ever-growing bank of qualitative and quantitative methods at your disposal, but most are built on a foundation of surveys, program tracking data, secondary data, focus groups, interviews, and observations. If those are the only six evaluation methods you ever know, you'll be in good shape. Let's examine each more closely:

Quantitative Data	Qualitative Data
Scale & Scope	*How & Why*
◆ Fixed-response survey questions ◆ Program tracking data	◆ Open-ended survey questions ◆ Focus groups ◆ Interviews ◆ Observations

Surveys

Surveys can generate both quantitative and qualitative data. Questions with pre-determined categories from which respondents are selecting one or more that apply to them, yield quantitative data, such as counts and numbers. Open-ended survey questions—also known as text boxes where you're not prepopulating responses, but letting respondents tell you what their experiences are from scratch—yield qualitative data.

Program Tracking Data

Let's say you want to track attendance figures for your program, that's quantitative data. For example, you might capture things like which sessions participants show up for, which instructor they had, whether or not they stayed for the whole period, what activities they participated in, and some demographic characteristics.

Secondary Data

Secondary data differs from program tracking data and survey data because you are not collecting it yourself. Someone else is collecting that data, and you are repurposing it for your own evaluation. For example, you can repurpose population-level health, poverty, or education statistics that are collected at the state, county, city, and zip code level, to justify the need for your programs or to monitor community-level changes over time.

Focus Groups and Interviews

Focus groups and interviews are very similar. Focus groups, in fact, are sometimes referred to as group interviews. Focus groups and interviews enable a conversation with your participants instead of handing them a predetermined survey. When you start to learn about a particular program experience, you can follow that experience and ask additional follow-up questions that help you build a rich story of what's happening. The difference between focus groups and interviews is how many people you're talking with at any one time. Interviews are one-on-one, and you have the opportunity go deeply with that person's particular experience. Focus groups tend to be between six and twelve people and explore the similarities and differences of experiences across participants. When deciding between focus groups and interviews, you want to think about how similar the participants are and the sensitivity of the topic. Are they going to have a similar enough experience that it makes sense for them to talk about it as a group? Is the topic one that people would feel comfortable sharing with strangers?

Observations

Observations allow you to collect data directly about things you can see happening. You should never be asking your participants something that you can observe for yourself. When using observations, you need a very carefully designed observation guide that outlines what it is you're looking for, and how to take notes on those observations. Observation data can help build up a rich picture of what's going on in the program for those who don't have an opportunity to experience it themselves.

What we have covered here is just enough for you to understand which types of data are best for which key evaluation questions. This is, of course, not enough information to actually conduct a good evaluation; it just skims the surface of what there is to know about each method. If you or someone on your team has an interest in learning more about any of these topics, there is a list of my favorite resources for each data source in **Appendix B.** In the next chapter, we'll cover the basics of how to execute these methods well.

Chapter Six

Executing the Evaluation

Now that we've covered the three steps of planning an evaluation, which are mapping your program, articulating your key evaluation questions, and matching your questions to the right evaluation methods, it's time to move into the two steps of doing an evaluation. In this chapter, we cover the critical considerations for executing an evaluation. In other words, designing instruments, collecting data, and analyzing that data. But this is not an evaluation methods textbook! There are many excellent resources already out there detailing how to write a survey or analyze qualitative data. See **Appendix B** for just a few suggestions. Each of those topics can and do fill a book.

The goal here is not to restate what other authors have already covered in such depth. Instead, we shift from the how-to of specific methods to focus on cross-cutting themes and considerations to help you execute evaluation in the real world, regardless of the methods you are using. I highlight common questions and pitfalls so you can increase the chances of your evaluation efforts going smoothly. First, we talk about the capacity needed to execute an evaluation and the timeline. Spoiler: you can't start an evaluation one month before the grant report is due. The second half of the chapter focuses on logistical considerations that, when overlooked, can wreak havoc on your carefully planned evaluation.

Capacity

Evaluation always takes more work than you think it will. I am firm believer that evaluation can work with a nonprofit executing it internally or with a nonprofit contracting with an external partner. But it is incredibly common for nonprofits to underestimate how much capacity it takes to do evaluation internally, and the evaluation learning curve takes time and practice. Because of the learning curve, it is a common path for nonprofits to transition from learning to do their own evaluation to having an external partner do their evaluation or some part of it. One of our local nonprofits was adamant about doing evaluation in-house, but once staff articulated key evaluation questions, they realized that keeping the work in-house would require the addition of a new staff person. The workload to learn how to do evaluation and then execute was beyond what any existing staff could absorb. Here are some suggestions for you to consider *before* you get into an evaluation to make sure you've lined up the right capacity to execute it:

Matching the Plan with Skills and Bandwidth

Once you have an evaluation plan, match that plan up with the skills and bandwidth necessary to execute it. Too often I find nonprofits assign staff to evaluation because of position or interest, without considering the specific skills needed to do the work. And again, I believe that all evaluation skills can be taught, but the amount of training necessary varies depending on the individual's starting point. It is much easier to train a former science major on quantitative analysis than someone who has not taken a math class since freshman year of college. The skills needed for secondary data and surveys are different than those for qualitative approaches. And the technical skills for data collection and analysis are different than the communication skills for reporting and helping the nonprofit learn from evaluation. You can learn more about this topic in **Chapter Seven.**

When identifying which staff members are best positioned to do or to support your evaluation, consider the overarching core competencies required to do an evaluation, which are endorsed by the American Evaluation Association.[7] Remember, qualitative data sources are especially labor intensive. For more details on options for staffing evaluation work, read **Chapter Eight.** Now let's pivot to participation, collaboration, and financials.

Who Participates? Everyone!

Someone needs to own the evaluation, but everyone needs to participate in the evaluation. The structure of the second half of this book, with a chapter for each position, is not an accident. There is a chapter for the development staff, communications staff, the executive director, the board, and the funders because each of those roles has a hand in evaluation. Without a

---

7 "American Evaluation Association Guiding Principles for Evaluation." June 7, 2018. https://www.eval.org/p/cm/ld/fid=51.

baseline understanding of evaluation and active engagement in the process throughout the nonprofit, the evaluation will suffer from the limitations outlined in **Chapter Two.** It will be a whole lot of work perceived as a waste because the evaluation did not answer the questions most important to the nonprofit. While everyone needs to participate, one person needs to own the evaluation. In my experience, having a committee or a team manage an evaluation is a fatal design flaw. Evaluation needs a champion who will serve as a single point of contact for the rest of the team and participants in the evaluation with whom to communicate.

Two Noggins Are Better than One

Two brains are always better than one, even if neither of you are experts in evaluation. One of the most prevalent mistakes I see in nonprofit evaluation is having a single person write a survey in a single take and sending it out to participants. Always, always, always have someone else read your instruments. Even if your reader knows nothing about evaluation, a second brain will catch obvious discrepancies, oversights, and things that just don't make sense. My now-husband reviewed many evaluation instruments when I was just starting out. Ask your second reader to review your instrument carefully and slowly from the perspective of whatever participant groups you serve. Even better, engage an active program participant to be your second reader.

Let's Not Forget the Financials

Each of the preceding tips pertains to human capacity, but we can't end this discussion without covering financial capacity. For too long, evaluation has been an expectation without a line-item. Nonprofits are expected to absorb the cost of evaluation needed to comply with funders' reporting requirements. Even if you are doing evaluation in-house, it still requires financing to cover staff time. If you take nothing else from this book, I hope you will grant yourself permission to start asking for the financial support that evaluation requires. I'll repeat myself on this point throughout this book because I think it is so important. If nonprofits are expected to do evaluation, it is reasonable to expect funding for the evaluation. A good rule of thumb is to add 10 percent of the program budget or $5,000, whichever is larger. If that number just sent you into a cold sweat, your nonprofit might not be ready for evaluation, and that's okay too. I find that unresourced evaluations are more harmful than no evaluation because they create the perception of knowledge based on shoddily designed, collected, or analyzed data.

Timelines

Like most things in the nonprofit field, evaluation takes more time than you think it will. The usual delays are multiplied in evaluation because evaluation is dependent on program implementation. Any delays associated with the program mirror the evaluation's progress and outcome. A month delay in recruiting beneficiaries also delays the evaluation a month... and sometimes more, because if it was difficult to get participants to sign up for the program, there's a good chance it will be hard to get them to participate in the evaluation.

Let me describe for you a project that was originally designed to be an evaluation of a six-month pilot program running from January to July 2017. Due to factors outside the control of the program, the start date was moved back by six months to July 2017. Then due to staff turnover, delays in getting partnerships up and running, and difficulty recruiting, the program did not actually start until October 2017. The program ran from October 2017 to May 2018, but the key evaluation questions the program staff prioritized were follow-up questions around whether the benefits of participating sustained after the program ended. Remember, you can read more about questions in **Chapter Four.** So, to match the key evaluation questions, the evaluation data collection happened in August 2018, with the final report delivered in October 2018. Instead of a six-month evaluation, contract extensions added up to a twenty-two-month evaluation! And with that, came added costs for the evaluation to cover maintaining ongoing check-ins between the program team and evaluation team for nearly four times longer than planned.

As a result of this experience and several other similar experiences, I'd like to suggest a few rules of thumb to save you the pain of learning these lessons firsthand:

Don't Mix Evaluation and Program Timelines

The evaluation timeline should never be the same as the program timeline. I recommend the evaluation planning starts a month before the program starts, though this is not always possible given grant award schedules. And I insist that the evaluation ends at least two months, preferably three, after the program ends. Post-program data collection happens at the end of the program. And then you need time to analyze and report that data. The situation is even more dire for programs curious about questions that require a longer period of follow-up, as in the example above. So, it makes

no sense that evaluation timelines end at the same time as the program…
and yet so often they do. Yes, this has implications for your grant report: if
the grant report requires final evaluation findings, it must be delayed and
that should be communicated to your funders as early as possible.

Data Collection Needs Space and Time

There is a natural limit on how quickly you can do data collection.
Evaluation can and should adapt to program and reporting timelines, but
at some point, the quality of the work suffers under too much compression.
And shrinking the timeline requires more hands on deck, which is not
always possible. I use the following "minimums" to build out timelines
before and after the program:

Task	Minimum Time	More if…
Evaluation Planning (**Chapters Three** and **Five**)	Six Weeks	◆ The planning group is a multipartner collaborative ◆ The program team's busyness delays the ability to review drafts
Instrument Design	Three Weeks	◆ Program team reviews in detail ◆ Many different instruments and complex topic
Data Collection: Surveys	Two Weeks	◆ The program is "low touch" and not high on participants' minds ◆ The time frame is busy for participants. See below for more.
Data Collection: Interviews, assuming ten plus and focus groups, assuming three plus	Four Weeks	◆ More interviews ◆ Longer interviews ◆ Limited windows of participant availability, such as working parents.

Data Collection: Program Tracking, Secondary Data, Observation	No additional time because it can happen during the program.	
Analysis and Reporting	Four Weeks	◆ Multiple reports or audiences ◆ High volume of data ◆ More than three data sources

Consider Cadence

Consider the cadence of your participants' lives. Your program and evaluation is not the only thing your participants are being asked to do. I know, shocker. An easy way to jeopardize your evaluation is to sync the data collection phase with really busy times for your participants. Working with teachers? Don't plan data collection at the end of the school year. Students? Don't send them a survey during standardized testing. Business professionals? Avoid the end of their fiscal year. These things seem obvious while you are reading this book right now, but in the chaos of program implementation and evaluation planning, nearly every program gets tunnel vision around when the data is "needed" and lose track of problematic times to ask participants to respond. Not only does this oversight threaten the quality of your data and lower your response rates, but it can also harm your relationships with participants. When you are insistent about collecting data at a certain time without recognizing your respondents' other commitments, they may decide that you and your program are out of touch with the people you are trying to serve.

Logistics

Throughout this section, we've hinted at the technical, interpersonal, and conceptual skills that evaluation requires. And now, we'll talk about the detail-oriented aspects of evaluation. Unfortunately, all the best evaluation thinking and planning can fall apart in the logistical details. What breaks my heart is that most are easy to fix; it's just that they are also easily overlooked. Since response rates are the most common logistical considerations nonprofits ask about, let's wrap up the chapter with a FAQ about them:

Should My Survey Be Electronic or Paper?

There's an old evaluation joke that if evaluators wrote a book of frequently asked evaluation questions, every page would say, "It depends."

Unfortunately, that is quite true in this case. Electronic surveys have become the default because of the ease and availability of online survey platforms, but they are not always the right fit. Which approach is going to be the easiest for your participants to access? Think about the computer and internet access of your participants. Think about their comfort level with technology. And think about the timing of when you want them to fill out surveys. Data collection with participants with sporadic internet access, older populations, and data collection right at the end of the program might lend itself better to paper surveys than electronic.

If you decide to go electronic, don't forget to optimize the survey for mobile access. At the time this book was written, mobile optimization was not the default on all survey platforms, so be sure to double check.

If you decide to go paper, formatting is important. A ten-page survey is intimidating even if it is only ten questions. My teams tries hard to format all paper surveys to no more than two pages, both sides.

Where Should I Conduct Interviews or Focus Groups?

Conduct interviews or focus groups wherever your participants are most comfortable. We are often asked to host focus groups for nonprofits at our offices. The answer is always *no* because beneficiaries don't know our offices. They don't know the location or the parking situation, and the surroundings aren't familiar. So much of the success of qualitative data collection is about the comfort level of participants, and location is a big part of that. Host your interviews and focus groups in the programming space that participants are familiar with.

Should I Record My Focus Groups and Interviews or Take Notes?

Whenever possible, audio record qualitative data collection, and be sure to gain consent from participants to do so. All smartphones have recording capabilities, or you can purchase a small recording device for less than $50. Transcription is so cheap and reliable these days that there is no reason to rely on notes for qualitative analysis or self-transcribe your recordings. After a lot of trial and error, the service my team uses is *Rev.com*, which costs $1 per minute of recording at the time of writing.

Now, I do not recommend video recording qualitative data collection. In my experience, participants ignore the audio recorder almost instantaneously, but the video recording is harder for some to tune out. It doesn't always change the dynamic, but to me the benefits of video over audio are negligible and the risks are substantial.

What Response Rate Should I Expect?

There is no universal target response rate. The response rate you should expect depends on the relationship you have built with participants and your history of using evaluation to improve the services they receive. Compare two nonprofits doing data collection the same month: first, we worked with a foundation with an explicit public focus on using evaluation to improve the processes and a history of behaving accordingly. We achieved a 100 percent response rate among the grantees included in the evaluation *in one week*. The foundation's strong relationship with grantees, and grantees' certainty that their feedback would be used meaningfully to improve the foundation's work, created an environment where participants were eager to respond.

In contrast, we worked with a nonprofit that had a more superficial relationship with a larger number of participants and while data was collected each year, participants remained skeptical that the nonprofit actually listened to and used their feedback. After five weeks of data collection, we were only able to generate responses from 4 percent of participants. The limited depth of the program engagement produced less engaged participants, further damaged by the perception that the nonprofit would not use their feedback.

How Many Respondents Do I Need to Make My Evaluation Valid?

Concerns about response rates often stem from questions like, "What sample size do we need for statistical significance?" The good news is that the vast majority of evaluation projects do not require statistical testing. Of the thirty evaluations that my team and I have conducted in the last year, four involved statistical testing. You only need to worry about statistical significance if your key evaluation questions require a comparison of two groups. Otherwise, you will only be conducting descriptive testing, and thus the sample size required is only the sample that will be compelling to your nonprofit and the audience of your evaluation. Read more about key evaluation questions in **Chapter Four.**

Two points on response targets:

My recommendation for survey response targets is to seek out similar programs to learn their response rates, set target numbers accordingly, and adjust each year based on your previous respondent counts.

For qualitative response targets, sample size is even less relevant, because the goal of qualitative data collection is to reach "satiation," the point at which you are not learning any new information. Studies have shown that the point of satiation occurs somewhere between six and twelve interviews.

How Do I Increase My Response Rates?

By the time you are asking how to increase your response rates, it's generally too late for that year, but you can take steps the following year to improve response rates. The best strategy for increasing response rates is to tangibly demonstrate to participants that their feedback is valued, heard, and used. The tool I have found that works best to increase response rates over time is the informative thank-you note outlined in **Chapter Seven.** In the short-term, three strategies can have small positive effects on response rates:

Say Yes to Incentives

Participants' data is theirs, and they should receive a tangible benefit for sharing it. My team finds Amazon gift cards particularly popular, though incentives need not be monetary. Other nonprofits have used early access to event registration or discounted registration, lunch with a field or nonprofit leader, and program swag. Think about what nonmonetary assets you have available that would be valuable to your beneficiaries. Providing incentives is more important than the specifics of which incentives you provide.

Send the Evaluation Request from a Trusted Staff Person

Nonprofits often want the evaluation recruitment to come from the evaluator, to maintain the third-party nature of the evaluation. I find that this can significantly decrease response rates. Even if you are working with an external evaluator, the request to participate should always come from the staff person the participant knows and trusts. Not the CEO, not the external evaluator.

Match the "Ask" to the Relationship

Be sure that you are making a reasonable ask given the benefit the participants receive from their involvement in the program. If your program is a one-hour drop-in program, asking for participants to agree to a one-hour interview is too much. If you're a funder granting $500,000 grants, you can ask for more participation in the evaluation than if you are granting $5,000. This is not an exact science, but it is worth pausing to consider if what you are asking participants is reasonable given the depth of their relationship with your program.

Chapter Seven

Getting the Most out of Reflection

Every few months I interact with nonprofits that have spent tens of thousands of dollars on evaluation and ended up with a very expensive paperweight. The evaluation process does not end when the data is in. The data alone can't make decisions about what actions to take. And data certainly can't take action to implement those decisions. That's where you come in: it is the nonprofit's leaders that take the data, identify what action, if any, the data requires, and take action to improve the nonprofit's services. Once you've taken the time to focus the evaluation on things that you care most about, like we discussed in **Chapters Three** through **Five,** and dedicated the resources to carrying the evaluation through as we explored in **Chapter Six,** the last step in the evaluation process is to reflect and learn.

This chapter is broken down into three sections and presented in the typical order when each occurs. We start with a discussion on how to make your written evaluation results as impactful as possible, then move into how to discuss them internally at your nonprofit and, finally, we conclude with tips on sharing evaluation results externally. By the end of this chapter, you have the tools you need to make sure that the evaluation translates into strategic decisions and no evaluation becomes a paperweight ever again.

In the evaluation field and at the time this book was written, there was a lot of chatter about nontraditional reporting formats. The typical logic goes: "Evaluation reports don't get used, so let's stop writing them. Instead, let's use short summaries and visual reports and infographics to communicate what we've learned." While I understand the sentiment, I'm not ready to give up on evaluation reports just yet. Instead of throwing the baby out with the bathwater, what are some changes that we can make to evaluation reports to make them more usable and valuable? I'd like to suggest two:

First, changes to the structure of the overall report and, second, changes to the structure of each section within the report. And if you'd like more information about nontraditional reporting formats, I'd recommend the Kauffman Foundation's "Evaluation Reporting Guide"[8] or Kylie Hutchinson's *A Short Primer on Innovative Evaluation Reporting*.[9] In addition to these two tips, I'd also encourage you to create an evaluation report in a PowerPoint deck instead of a Word document: showing one slide at a time helps you zero in on each point you are trying to make and keeps the reader's attention on that point in a way that a Word document can't. Let's talk about grouping your information so readers and listeners grasp your a-ha findings more easily.

Structure Your Results for Greater Impact

Because much of the evaluation process overlaps with research, the field also borrowed the reporting structure used by researchers: introduction, methodology, results, findings, and discussion. Now imagine reading a report like that. You have to wade through pages and pages of details about the evaluation process before ever getting to the meat of the learnings. By that point, most of us have zoned out and *never* get to the learnings!

Evaluation reports should flip the research report script: start with a summary of the findings, then follow with the detailed learnings for each key evaluation question and, finally, put the methodology and demographics in the very back. I do still include a general introduction section at the beginning to orient readers. The most important element is to sort your findings by key evaluation question so that readers can find the information that they care most about quickly and easily. Traditionally, research reports sort findings by method: they present the survey findings and then the interview findings separately. This approach leaves the synthesis to the reader and increases the barriers to reading and using the report. Instead, pull all of the findings related to a certain question into the same section, regardless of what method they came from. After you process these visual examples, let's review some common mistakes to avoid in the next section.

---

8 Ewing Marion Kauffman Foundation, "Evaluation Reporting Guide," https://www.kauffman.org/evaluation/evaluation-reporting-guide

9 Hutchison, Kylie. Gibsons: Community Solutions Planning & Evaluation, 2017.

Sample Evaluation Report

Insights start on page 10

Table of Contents

Sample Research Report

Insights start on page 79

Table of Contents

No-Nos and Data Sandwiches

Another report no-no I see constantly in nonprofit evaluation reports is what I call "data vomit." Data vomit is when you take a bunch of random data and evaluation findings and throw them at random throughout a report without any context or interpretation. I see this approach most often in bulleted lists in grant reports, and it looks something like:

Because of your attendance at the event, which of the following you do plan to do? (n = 181)

◆ Use resources or tools received at the event: 150 (83 percent)

◆ Follow up with new contacts: 71 (39 percent)

◆ Reconnect with colleagues: 56 (31 percent)

◆ Share stories: 48 (27 percent)

This technique, again, puts the burden on the reader to determine why those numbers matter and the majority of the time, especially when you're working with folks who aren't naturally inclined towards evaluation, the answer is that it doesn't matter to them. A better strategy is what I call a "data sandwich." A data sandwich has three parts: a conclusion, the supporting data, and a pretty picture.

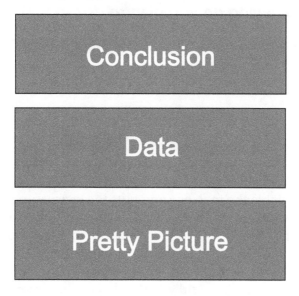

First, share one sentence about what you took away from the data, which is the conclusion. In the example above, the sentence might be, "Attendees were most likely to use resources or tools as a result of the event." The second sentence should support your conclusion with data. In this case, "In fact, 83 percent of attendees reported that as a result of the event, they planned to use resources or tools received at the event. The next most common follow-up action, follow up with new contacts, was selected by only 39 percent of attendees."

The last element is a pretty picture related to your finding so readers who are visual learners or who want to see the full supporting data can do so easily. If your data is quantitative, you will most likely have a chart or graph. If your data is qualitative, you'll have to be more creative about how to present key themes in a visual way, or you can start with a simple quote box. The full data sandwich then reads:

Attendees were most likely to use resources or tools as a result of the event. In fact, 83 percent of attendees reported that as a result of the event, they planned to use resources or tools received that were provided. The next most commonly reported action, meaning follow up with new contacts, was selected by only 39 percent of attendees.

Because of your attendance at the event, which of the following do you plan to do? (n = 181)

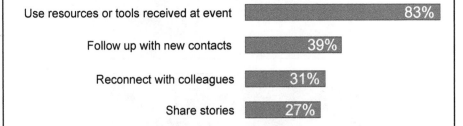

Compare the data sandwich to the original data vomit: the data sandwich highlights the message and puts the legwork in the hands of the writer instead of the reader. Each data sandwich should include only one finding, though one finding might encompass multiple sources of data. In the example above, if we had qualitative data on what specific resources and tools were most useful, we might include that in the same sandwich. And you should only have sandwiches for things that will matter most to your reader: in other words, results that answer your key evaluation questions. For example, you don't need a data sandwich to talk about the demographics of your respondents, and that information should be at the end of your report. Now that we've covered sandwiches, we can talk about digesting your findings before you celebrate results.

Talking Results: Helping Others Understand and Learn

After you've digested your evaluation findings and written them up, you're ready to share your results and talk about them. You're excited because you've learned a great deal, so you share the results by email to everyone on your team... and hear nothing back. Because useful evaluation is still a new thing to most of your colleagues, it takes a little bit more hand-holding to help them read, understand, and learn from the evaluation. In this section, we'll walk through the strategies that I use most often to talk with others about evaluation results:

Field Tested: The Data Sandwich

I regularly offer training on all sorts of evaluation topics and, consistently, participants tell me that data sandwiches are the most useful tip they learn among any of my training topics. They provide a simple way to structure reporting data that makes a big difference in your ability to communicate it clearly. The nonprofits who have made the transition to data sandwiches confirm that they are a hit with funders, donors, boards, and internal audiences of all sorts.

Data Parties

My favorite way to engage staff in a discussion about evaluation results is by scheduling a "data party." In this section, I paint the overall picture of what a data party looks like and then suggest some more specific "level two" resources you can try.

I recommend bringing together your front-line program staff with the staff responsible for the evaluation, and a few members of the leadership team for a minimum of two hours. Having the whole leadership team present can sometimes stifle discussion about not-so-positive findings, so use your judgment. This is also not the time to include your board. There are tips for when and how to share evaluation results with board members later in this chapter and in **Chapter Eleven.** This is your opportunity to dive into what the data means, use the data to set goals for the next year, and celebrate program successes. Don't worry too much at this point about doing the learning session "right." The important part is getting in the habit of discussing data together. Get some food, some flip chart paper, and dive into your evaluation results.

The best way I have found to approach this discussion is to use "What?— So What?—Now What?" as a guiding framework. In other words, you first discuss, "What?"

◆ What are the results from each data source?

◆ How do the data sources fit together?

◆ What are the points of agreement and disagreement across sources?

In this phase, the discussion should be purely factual, making sure that everyone in the room understands the evaluation data. Then you move on to, "So What?"

◆ What does the data mean and why do we care?

◆ How does each person in the room interpret the data?

◆ If you had to summarize answers to each key evaluation question in one sentence, what would it be?

◆ What areas emerge as top program successes?

◆ What areas emerge as potential areas for improvement?

The "So What?" phase is where interpretation and context get layered on top of the data. For example, we recently worked with a nonprofit that had outstanding results except for one outcome area. In that outcome area, survey results indicated that just over 50 percent of participants experienced an improvement, compared to around 90 percent of participants for all other outcome areas. My team thought that represented a failure of one part of programming.

But, when my team presented those numbers to the program staff, they were thrilled! To them, half of participants experiencing improvement was tremendous, because in the year before only 30 percent of participants experienced improvement in this area, and because it was a really hard area to change. We agreed on the "what" of the data, but our "so what" differed. As a result of this conversation with the program team, we were able to reframe the way the data was presented and strengthen the written evaluation report. The last step is to discuss, "Now What?"

◆ What comes next?

◆ What do we need to make sure to maintain about the program?

◆ What tweaks should we try to implement?

◆ What topics do we need to learn more about next year?

"Now What?" is your opportunity to move from backward-looking evaluation to forward-looking planning. It can be hard to resist the urge to jump to the "Now What?" early in the conversation. We've found that holding off until you've been through the "What?" and "So What?" helps ensure all staff members feel heard, included and, in the end, produce action plans that are more fully informed by the full picture the data paints.

All data parties should follow the basic "What?—So What?—Now What?" structure, but there are some helpful tools and aids that can make the conversation more grounded in the evaluation data. I'll share three of my favorites here:

The Gallery Walk

The first data party aid we will discuss is a gallery walk, a strategy adapted from teachers in classroom settings. Before you begin the data party, create posters displaying a different set of data or findings and hang them on the wall throughout your meeting space. During the data party, you can approach a gallery walk in an unstructured way, letting participants wander through the posters on their own, the same way they might navigate an art gallery. Or, you can structure the walk by splitting participants into small groups and rotating around each poster for a fixed time period.

Regardless of which strategy you take, it is critical that each participant spends time with every poster and that there is some tool for participants to capture their reactions in real time. Consider using either a private reflection form or having participants post sticky notes with reflections on the edges of the poster. Remember the "What?—So What?—Now What?" structure? Perhaps use different colored sticky notes for reflections in each category or create a reflection form that has sections for each step. Once all participants have had time with every poster, come back together for a group discussion using the reflection questions from the previous section.

At this point, everyone has reflected on the specific data sections, so the conversation should focus on bringing all the threads together.

Gallery walks are a great strategy for large groups when you have a large space to move around. But because participants are interacting with data independently, it requires that participants have some preexisting understanding of how to interpret data. Thus, it can often be better to start with one of the next two strategies, or a data party without an aid, before introducing the gallery-walk technique.

Data Placemats

The second data party aid I recommend trying is using data placemats to visualize key data or findings. Before the data party, the evaluator prepares the preliminary findings from the analysis using visualizations. If you refer to the early passage in this chapter about data sandwiches, the goal here is to only include the "pretty picture" on the placemat. The data party then determines the conclusion. The goal is to have one to three 11" by 17" pages. More than that is too much for one data party, so be selective about the data you are presenting. Think about your key evaluation questions and the most critical data for each question. Think about the data that would benefit most from program staff interpretation. In addition to data visualizations, there should also be space below each section for participants to take notes. Nothing is more frustrating than a placemat you can't scribble on.

During the data party, facilitate the "What?—So What?—Now What?" conversation using the placemats as a guide. Go section by section as a group and pull out key findings and the story or context behind them. Ask what surprises participants, and what factors might explain the trends. The goal is to take the static data and contextualize the findings.

Data placemats are a great strategy when the program staff have specific contextual understanding of the project and a willingness to engage with data. This approach works best with groups of less than ten people to facilitate a rich discussion. But this strategy also requires a project with time and capacity for participatory approaches during the analysis phase. Compared to the other aids I recommend, data placemats use half-baked analysis—just the pretty pictures, not the conclusions. So, the evaluator has to do another round of work after the data party to create a report following the suggestions presented earlier in this chapter and incorporating the context shared during the data party. Not all projects can accommodate that additional step.

The Guessing Game

The final data party aid I suggest you explore is creating a guessing game with the results. Using this approach, you ask participants to guess what they think the results will show before they see the data and use those guesses to start the conversation. You need not have participants submit or share their guesses. Rather, I've found it works well for each individual to come prepared with guesses and the reasons for those guesses. Once you're together, discuss as a group where expectations were met, surpassed, or unmet after the data is revealed. I've seen some dramatic strategies to reveal the data, including scratch-off cards and "Price is Right" style prizes for the participant who gets closest to the actual results. These can be fun but are not necessary to make the guessing game work.

The guessing game strategy is great for participants who have not engaged extensively with data in the past, because it forces them to put some thought into what they expect and why before introducing the data. It doesn't take much advance work on the evaluator's part, but it does require participants who will commit to some pre-thinking before the data party.

These suggestions are just to get you started. There is an endless and growing list of participatory approaches to engaging staff in discussions about data. The most important part is that you try something: host a data party and use "What?—So What?—Now What?" to guide your discussion. From there, you can start to incorporate some of the fancier aids I've outlined here.

Negative Data: How to Support the Staff

Before we end our discussion on sharing evaluation results, I want to address one of the hardest parts of evaluation: how to handle negative findings. It's important to remember that even when you have framed evaluation as a learning process from the beginning, the results are still emotionally charged for staff members who have poured their hearts into the work. Negative findings can be tough and reactions to them can be unpredictable.

I'll give you two examples to illustrate my point:

In the first example, a nonprofit hired my team to conduct an evaluation of a pilot early childhood program. It was the first time running the program, so you would expect more room for improvement than perfection. But when we finished the analysis and prepared for the data party, we were blown away by the balance of positive results. Overall, participants seemed changed by the program, and areas for improvement were minor and easy to fix. We went into the data party excited to share these positive findings, and within fifteen minutes the program director, Sarah, was in tears.

Apparently, this program was Sarah's baby, what she had been working her whole career to create, and she was not at all prepared to hear anything negative about it. We were caught completely off guard. A common phrase we use is "no evaluation is ever all positive or all negative," and this evaluation was heavily skewed toward the positive side compared to most other projects we experienced. But Sarah didn't have that context. This was her first major program evaluation and the negative components felt deeply personal to her. Luckily for us, Sarah's direct supervisor, Raquel, was also at the data party and stepped in to reassure Sarah that on balance, this was an extremely positive evaluation she should be proud of and the rest of the team was proud of her.

On a different occasion, my team was asked to conduct an evaluation of equity and inclusion across the nonprofit. The topic was emotionally charged from the start and the results were not favorable. There were some specific negative findings about specific decisions and people within the nonprofit, including the HR director, Jacob, who would be at our data party. My team spent hours thinking and talking through how to best present these less-than-glowing results. We showed up for the data party nervous but prepared. And much to our surprise, the response to the negative findings was overwhelmingly positive. Instead of getting defensive, Jacob appreciated having tangible documentation of the areas that needed improvement. To him, the evaluation took these issues from the shadows to the forefront where he was empowered to do something about them. In reflecting on the conversation afterward with our main point of contact, Viraj, it became clear that two factors influenced the unexpected reaction.

First, the nonprofit staff knew something was going on, but exactly what wasn't clear. The negative results were not a surprise to them. The team hired us because they expected negative results but needed external validation and additional details on what wasn't working and why. Second, the evaluation never fell off the nonprofit's radar. In many of our projects, we go through the planning as summarized in **Chapters Three** to **Five.** Then we disappear to do the evaluation and we pop back in with the results. Half of the attendees at the data party haven't thought about evaluation in six months since we began our engagement.

In this nonprofit, Viraj was sharing our evaluation updates with the executive team at their bi-weekly meetings throughout the project. He was also using that time to set expectations for the evaluation results and what would come after the evaluation. By the time we returned for the data party, nonprofit staff were ready to jump into action, and just needed guidance on where to direct that action. As these two examples demonstrate, there is no silver bullet or "right way" to present negative findings. So much depends on the culture of the nonprofit, the temperament of the individuals involved, and expectations for the evaluation. Here are four strategies that I have found to be successful over the years:

How to Handle Findings

Be strategic on how and if you share findings in advance of the data party. I have found that when results are sensitive, it is preferable *not* to share results in advance. When the findings are negative and personal, the individuals affected have a tendency to work themselves up about them and come into the room defensive.

Surprises Are Best for Birthdays

Now, some individuals don't like to be surprised and want time to digest in advance. In these cases, I recommend sharing only with a small group— maybe just the executive who is most supportive of the evaluation. In that way, you can recruit someone else to help handle any unexpected reactions, like Raquel did for us, without letting preemptive defensiveness run wild.

Choose This Method for Negative Findings

The guessing game aid works great for circumstances where negative findings are prevalent. Front-line staff members usually have a gut feeling about how things are working, and I have found they often guess that things are more negative than the evaluation showed. Even if leadership guesses more positively, having the perspective of front-line staff to balance expectations is helpful. Sometimes my team asks for guesses to be submitted in advance, so they can tailor their approach to align with the group's expectations.

Managing Expectations

Hold a pre-meeting with your colleagues to discuss what you expect from the evaluation, which is typically a mix of good and bad, and what is expected after the evaluation—action, not self-criticism— like Viraj did.

Remember that none of these suggestions has worked in every scenario. The best advice I can give you is to be prepared for the negative from the start. Have regular conversations with the whole nonprofit about your expectations that the evaluation will reveal a mix of results to make you proud and areas that need some work. And be empathetic to your colleagues—and yourself—when negative findings arise. You all do this work because you care and respond emotionally to negative findings because the staff care. Be sensitive, supportive, and understanding.

Share Your Evaluation Results With Three Groups

Once you have discussed the evaluation internally, it's time to start sharing. Far too many evaluations end up in a file cabinet and never see the light beyond the staff who worked on it. I believe this is not rooted in malice, but unawareness of how nonprofits can and should share evaluation results. There are three groups that I would recommend you share evaluation results with: your direct beneficiaries, your board, and your broader audience.

Share with Your Beneficiaries

One of my favorite evaluation tools is not evaluation at all, but communication: I call it an informative thank-you note. Instead of asking your beneficiaries to participate in evaluation and have that information go into a black box that they never hear about again, close the feedback loop. It's an opportunity to share what you learned from your beneficiaries and what you are planning to do with that information. I believe that informative thank-you notes are a critical piece of evaluation because:

◆ Ethically, data belong to the people who share it, and they have a right to know how you are using what's collected. Yes, you should share how you *plan* to use data when you ask for the data, but beneficiaries also have a right to know how the data is *actually* used.

◆ Evaluation is an extension of a nonprofit program. Beneficiaries do not distinguish between evaluation and your program. So, if you value positive and transparent relationships with beneficiaries, that approach should extend to your evaluation.

◆ Feedback is informing programming choices and increases the likelihood that participants will share feedback in the future. Sending informative thank-you notes is the single best strategy I have found to increase evaluation response rates.

◆ They provide another opportunity for feedback. I have seen cases where a beneficiary had a really different experience with a program than the evaluation uncovered. The beneficiary did not participate in the original evaluation, but when the informative thank-you note arrived, the beneficiary responded to share about a divergent experience. In this way, the nonprofit had a fuller picture of what was happening in its program because it took the time to close the feedback loop.

Informative Thank-You Note Template

I wanted to take this moment to sincerely thank you for participating in the evaluation [or survey/interviews/focus groups/feedback process] for the [program name]. XX percent of this year's [volunteers/teachers/participants] provided feedback. We, at [program name], have learned so much from you and wanted to share some of what we gathered and how we plan to respond to those learnings.

◆ Learning #1 - For example, 95 percent of you are satisfied with the program so far this year.

◆ Learning #2 - For example, 83 percent of you are satisfied with your reader.

◆ Learning #3 - For example, 87 percent of you are satisfied with the support you receive from staff.

◆ We learned that [insert example of positive kudos that you heard on the survey]

◆ But we also learned we have room to grow and improve. For example, [insert a general summary of issues]

In response to these learnings, we are working to: [insert a general statement of how you are going to adapt to this feedback]

If you have had other findings that you would like to share with us, please feel free! It would be great to hear from you. Look out for another feedback opportunity [insert next survey, or focus group opportunity, if applicable, and approximate date]

Signed,

[the staff who beneficiaries interact with most]

and

[the executive director]

Now that you are sold on sending informative thank-you notes, how do you go about it? The first step is to internally figure out what the data say and mean, following the "What?—So What?—Now What?" approach detailed earlier in this chapter. Then, prepare an informative thank-you note with the template on the prior page. There is no need to summarize all results or include particularly negative or outlying feedback. The goal is to let beneficiaries know that you hear them, you appreciate them, and you are using their feedback to improve the services they receive. Send it to everyone you asked to participate in the evaluation, *not just those who did participate.* And share as soon as possible—you want beneficiaries to still remember the evaluation you are referencing.

Share with the Board

The next audience to share evaluation results with is your board of directors. **Chapter Eleven** is entirely devoted to how boards can engage productively with evaluation—I recommend you read that chapter in full before venturing into evaluation conversations at the board level. The overall guidance on sharing with your board is that boards need their own version of the evaluation presentation. The level of detail at the data party is too much for most boards because their role involves higher-level policy decisions. I would strongly caution against having a board member in the room for the data party because it changes the dynamic, often in an unproductive way that limits conversation. And the level of detail that you share with beneficiaries is not detailed enough. The board needs to hear the good, bad, and ugly to be a productive partner in evaluation work.

My advice on sharing evaluation with the board is to share all three parts of the "What?—So What?—Now What?" formula. Share not only the positive and negative, but also share both with a clear plan of action for what comes next. Tell the board that evaluation was not just for show, but is an important strategic tool for the nonprofit to do its best work. Use the reflection questions in **Chapter Eleven** as a way to engage the board in a productive conversation about the results, and to strengthen their commitment to evaluation for future years. Approach the presentation as a two-way discussion, rather than a one-way update.

Share with Your Broader Audience

Lastly, I hope you will consider sharing your evaluation reports or a summary version on your website and perhaps in your newsletter. The more opportunities you provide your audience to interact with evaluation, the more likely it is the nonprofit has the support, financial and otherwise, to sustain evaluation work. And sharing evaluation results publicly is one of the best signs of whether a nonprofit is truly and deeply committed to learning for two reasons:

Emphasis on Learning

Public dissemination demonstrates that the nonprofit authentically believes evaluation is for learning. If learning isn't the priority, the nonprofit would only share positive evaluation findings. Sharing all evaluation findings puts your money where your mouth is and clearly says to the world, we value all of these learnings, not just the positive ones. In fact, explicitly prefacing public-facing evaluation results with context about evaluation's role as a learning tool can help set the stage for the reader.

Share Findings with Your Peers

Public dissemination extends the learning opportunity to the broader field. Remember in **Chapter Four** when I suggested that you look to learn from others when you're deciding where to focus your evaluation? During the writing of this book, that's really hard to do because so few nonprofits share their results. The problem is especially acute for things you find that don't work as well as you hoped. In research-speak, we call this the "file drawer problem": positive findings that support a program are pushed for publication and dissemination, findings that aren't as positive get put in a file drawer. More and more, we are seeing foundations lead the way in sharing the good and the bad through "fail fest" events.

A Word on Sharing

Sharing results publicly does not mean that you share the same version of the report you use internally. That report was created for an internal audience and what's appropriate for an external audience looks a little bit different. In particular, I recommend creating a summary report of the evaluation findings, good and not so good, and then adding a section on reflections, implications, and plans for addressing the learnings.

Part Three

Pick Your Position: How Evaluation Can Work for You

There is a temptation to force evaluation into one staff member's role and responsibilities. But it doesn't work like that. Evaluation cuts across the nonprofit and needs the engagement of every staff member. You can think of evaluation like human anatomy. The five evaluation steps we covered in **Part Two** make up the spine, providing the structure for successful evaluation work. Now in **Part Three,** we examine the head and four limbs that make evaluation work move forward.

Here are the head and limbs of evaluation and the functions they fulfill:

◆ Without the engagement of the *executive director*, the evaluation loses sight of the big picture and misses its connection the nonprofit's larger purpose. Think of the executive director as the head of the evaluation anatomy, sitting atop the body to orchestrate coordinated movement, but not doing the heavy lifting.

◆ The heavy lifting of taking the evaluation and sharing it with the world lies with *the communications staff and the development staff.* Think of these two functions as the arms of our evaluation anatomy, able to gather suggestions from the outside world and share their own findings.

◆ *The board of directors and foundations* round out our evaluation anatomy, providing a base of support as the legs. Without their full endorsement, evaluation can still make slow, plodding forward progress. But with their engagement, evaluation can move in leaps and bounds.

What About Program Staff?

You will notice there is not a specific chapter for program staff. In my experience, program staff have a presence throughout this entire book. Rather than functioning as a part of the evaluation anatomy, the program staff members are the veins, arteries, and nerves flowing throughout. Without a program, there is no evaluation. You will find tips applicable to your program team in each and every chapter in this book. I also address the program staff in **Part Four.**

You need not read this entire section in order. Pick the chapter that applies best to you and start there. If another chapter sounds intriguing, read that too, since we know that nonprofit workload tends to trickle over. Then pass the book along to a colleague in a different role. By the time the nonprofit has finished this section, you will all have a better idea of how your contributions come together to make the most of evaluation.

Chapter Eight

The Executive Director

In this chapter, we zero in on what executive directors need to understand to engage productively with evaluation. First, we discuss how executive directors can use evaluation to better understand their team. Second, we examine how executive directors can promote evaluation of their programs. While it's rare for executive directors to take lead responsibility for evaluation, without their support and active engagement, evaluation efforts falter. The most important evaluation-related roles for the executive director are to build evaluation into the fabric of the nonprofit, staff evaluation appropriately whether using internal or external expertise, and continuously beat the drum of evaluation as a learning tool for internal and external communications.

As the executive director of a nonprofit, you wear many hats. You're responsible for building, supporting, and managing the staff. And that role requires you know a little bit about every part of the nonprofit, from programming to events planning to operations. You're responsible to the board, but also responsible for managing the board, and cultivating strong relationships while continuing to support board development. You oversee funding, and even if you have a development team, you still play a leading role in cultivating major donors and maintaining key foundation relationships. And you're accountable for serving your community with the best, most effective programming possible, which is, after all, why you are so devoted to your other areas of responsibility. Just thinking about all of those essential tasks wears me out, and I can only imagine the exhaustion that comes with executing the work week after week under the constant pressure of maintaining exceptional financial performance. How do you ever find space to fit evaluation in?

Fortunately, there's already room for evaluation. If you start to listen for it, you'll hear undertones of evaluation in your conversations. Supporting staff require an understanding of the components of effective programming and having good evaluation results can help inform those hard decisions about resource allocation. The board is there to provide oversight and ensure that the nonprofit is serving the community, which only evaluation can answer. And funders and donors want to know their money is going toward something that genuinely has an impact—again, a question for evaluation. My contention is that while it takes some time and energy to shift your focus to evaluation, in the long-term that shift can actually make the rest of your job easier. And I don't base this contention on hopes and dreams and fairy dust, but on real-world experience where I've seen this shift happen.

Love Over Hate

Let's look at Felix's scenario. He's the executive director of a nonprofit called Love Over Hate. When I met Felix, he was six months into his role as executive director after eleven years in increasingly senior programming roles within the nonprofit. Felix had high hopes for what Love Over Hate could be and dreamed of major improvements in most of his key areas of responsibility. One of the areas Felix was hoping to start with was beefing up Love Over Hate's evaluation efforts. The nonprofit had always done some form of evaluation, but to Felix it never felt worth the effort it took. He knew in his gut that evaluation could be the key to informing the other major changes he hoped to make, but he wasn't sure how. He'd heard of nonprofits with the meaningful evaluation he wanted, but he hadn't seen one up close. They were like rumors of unicorns. Through pure luck, I met a member of Felix's board through another business engagement. The board member immediately introduced me to Felix, and in our first meeting it was clear that we shared the same optimism for the power of evaluation when done collaboratively and with a learning focus.

Over the next year, I had the opportunity to work closely with Felix and witness how evaluation transformed Love Over Hate. It wasn't easy at first. In particular, there was stronger staff resistance to an increased focus on evaluation than Felix anticipated. But over time, evaluation provided a neutral launching point to discuss and justify the other key decisions facing the nonprofit.

One tangible example was Felix's struggle with upgrading the database systems. Funders and staff were split on whether the systems were fine as is or needed a major overhaul. In his previous program role, Felix thought the database didn't need upgrading. As an executive director, evaluation changed his mind and broke the tie for funders and staff: once Love Over Hate had articulated key evaluation questions and designed an evaluation to answer those questions, it was clear that the current database could not support what the evaluation needed and the answers it would provide. With that clarity, Felix found that funders, even those who were previously resistant, were instantly supportive of the expense.

In the second half of this chapter, I present some of the main lessons that helped Felix use evaluation to make other areas of his job easier. But first, let's briefly discuss how executive directors use evaluation to measure their internal team's performance in a way that both parties will appreciate.

Evaluating Your Internal Team

When I interact with executive directors new to the nonprofit space, their assumption is that when I talk about evaluation, I mean personnel evaluation and performance reviews. While performance reviews are not the focus of this book, I offer three tips, none of which will be surprising if you've read **Part Two,** to clear your mind.

Performance Review Systems

Nonprofits spend a lot of time and energy finding the "right" performance management system. They spend months comparing and contrasting SuccessFactors and PeopleSoft. But it's not the system that matters, it's the conversation. Similar to the process for program evaluation outlined in **Part Two,** staff should be deeply involved in developing their performance goals, selecting what to track for evidence of performance on those goals, and reflecting on the similarities and differences between the goals and their performance at certain points in time. The system itself is just a place to store the selected goals and evidence of progress and to create company-wide check-in points. For a small nonprofit, this might be equally achievable with a spreadsheet and calendar alerts. *The emphasis in performance reviews should be on the process, not the storage solution.*

Performance Review Measures

Remember our conversation in **Chapter Five** about how there is not one "best" data source, but there are different types of data best for different key evaluation questions? The same applies to performance reviews. Not all employee roles lend themselves to nice clean quantitative performance measures like fundraising goals. My team and I recently worked on an evaluation project that intersected with performance reviews. The board of directors of a membership association had set goals for staff and based their annual bonuses on achievement of those goals. The board insisted that all goals were measured on the same quantitative scale, but not all the goals lent themselves to the same quantitative scale.

One goal was response time: do the staff respond to members within twenty-four hours? Another goal was relevancy: do members perceive the programming as relevant to their work? The former is pretty easy to quantify, but the latter is more difficult. Putting both on the same scale put members in a position where they could easily answer about response time, but the relevancy question did not make as much sense and their responses were variable and inconsistent even between different questions on the same survey. The difficulty of using the scale had a pernicious unintended consequence: the front-line team who responded to member inquiries received their bonus more regularly than the behind the scenes team who planned program content due purely to the way their goals were measured.

The year we worked with the membership nonprofit, we educated the executive team and the board on the importance of matching the measure to the goal. With our revised tool that used both a new quantitative scale and qualitative data to capture relevancy, both the front-line team and the program planning team received a more accurate performance rating and fair bonus allocation.

Framing Performance Reviews

My last tip is to frame performance reviews as an opportunity to learn and grow first, and as a punitive accountability tool only when that becomes necessary. Staff are more likely to engage with the performance review process if it is presented as something that can support their growth. If it is seen as having only potential downside, you'll end up with a review that highlights only the good and you might miss an opportunity to support your team because the challenge was left undisclosed out of fear of repercussions. I know when team members are not carrying their weight that the conversation must focus on improvement or termination. But this is the minority of cases and should not drive the overall performance management process.

Embedding Program Evaluation Into the Nonprofit

The remainder of this chapter will focus on how executive directors can most effectively build evaluation into their nonprofits. In this chapter,

I talk about decisions that fall directly onto the executive director. But there are other areas, like development, working with the board, and communications, in which you might play a supporting role. I'd recommend you read the rest of this chapter first, and then consider reading the chapters intended for other positions on your staff. Those passages will further support your efforts to build program evaluation into the nonprofit. Let's take a closer look at how Felix focused on re-educating his team.

From Performance Reviews to Program Evaluation

Staff who are new to the nonprofit world may believe the same myth that evaluation equals performance reviews. Part of your role as the executive director might be to re-educate them on the differences. The main way that program evaluation differs from staff performance review is the locus of control. In general, the areas on which staff members are evaluated are largely under the control of the staff member. There are always going to be larger contextual factors, such as financial downturns or drop-in donations, but there is a stronger causal link between staff actions and staff performance. Programs are more complicated. On one hand, the responsibility for a program tends to be distributed across a larger group of people, sometimes including partners outside the nonprofit. On the other, as we've discussed throughout this book, social outcomes are hard to change and influenced by an array of factors outside the program that your nonprofit delivers. There is not a clear and singular causal link between the program and participant performance.

Staffing Evaluation

One of the most important decisions the executive director makes is how to staff evaluation. Once a nonprofit decides to move forward with evaluation, it has to be someone's job responsibility or it will not happen. There are three options for staffing evaluation: add evaluation to an existing staff member's role or

Set the Stage Like Felix

When Felix from Love Over Hate started to talk to his team about implementing a more intensive evaluation process, he discussed it in the context of team effort that the full staff were responsible for, not just the program team. And he also framed evaluation as a learning effort, emphasizing that jobs weren't on the line based on evaluation results, but instead that reactions to the evaluation results—meaning, how staff adopted those learnings and applied them to their jobs—would become a piece of their performance reviews in all future years.

distribute it across current staff members, hire an internal evaluator to join your team, or contract with an external evaluator. There are pros and cons to all three approaches, and in this section, I'll share tips for making whichever option you choose as successful as possible.

	Pros	Cons
Existing Staff	Integration of evaluation into the nonprofit	Lack of focus on and skills for evaluation
Internal Evaluator	Focus and attention on evaluation with integration into the nonprofit	Ill-defined, improperly salaried position leads to frequent turnover
External Evaluator	High-level expertise within budget	Evaluation remains peripheral to the nonprofit's core functions

Adding Evaluation to an Existing Staff Role

The first approach to staffing evaluation is to assign evaluation responsibilities to one or more existing staff roles. Most often, I see executive directors asking program staff or development staff to take on responsibility for the evaluation function. When successful, this approach works well because it can strengthen the alignment between programs and evaluation and ensure that evaluation is built into the fabric of the nonprofit. But the risk is that evaluation will always play second fiddle to the staff member's other responsibilities and that the staff lack the evaluation skills necessary to implement it well.

I have seen examples of this approach working well and not working at all. In the nonprofit that it worked well, the executive director of a seven-person nonprofit chose to make evaluation part of everyone's job, with ultimate responsibility for the evaluation resting with the executive director. In this case, the nonprofit invested in extensive evaluation capacity building through trainings and coaching to build the evaluation knowledge base of the staff. Every staff member was required to participate, and over time, we saw individual staff members taking an interest in different components of the evaluation and becoming true experts in those aspects.

Today, the nonprofit has one staff member responsible for all qualitative aspects of the evaluation, one staff member who takes the lead on surveys, and one who maintains the administrative tracking data. Some staff members never took to evaluation, and while they are still responsible for participating in evaluation planning and reflection, they are no longer required to execute any part of the evaluation. The executive director maintains responsibility for overseeing the whole evaluation process and ensuring that the learning cycles outlined in **Chapter Seven** continue. And the set-up is working well for them. No one staff member is drowning under the weight of responsibility for the full evaluation, and the whole nonprofit is productively engaged in evaluation as a core function of the work.

On the other hand, I have seen examples where embedding evaluation into existing staff roles has failed catastrophically. In one nonprofit I partnered with, a member of the program staff approached the executive director about increasing the nonprofit's focus on evaluation. The executive director responded with, "Okay, you do it" and reformulated her job description to focus on evaluation. In fact, within a week the executive director had changed the staff member's job title from director of programs to director of evaluation. The new director of evaluation sought out coaching for the new evaluation role, first informally from others in a similar position and then formally with me. But the situation was plagued from the start with a number of challenges.

First, while the new director of evaluation has an interest in evaluation, training in evaluation was lacking. And to make matters worse, the program worked in a complex and long-term arena of funding basic research, so the evaluation was equally complex and long-term, and needed a creative, expert evaluator. The executive director expected the staff member to be able to jump right into evaluation and lead the nonprofit in that space, without giving her time to learn and adjust.

Second, the executive director was never truly bought into the focus on evaluation. After the fact, it became clear that the redefinition of the staff role was driven by a fear of losing that staff member rather than agreement that evaluation was the right direction for the nonprofit. And third, despite the title change, program responsibilities were not reallocated. The director of evaluation was continually asked to contribute to her previous responsibilities, further muddying the water and delaying her ability to learn necessary evaluation skills. A little more than a year after the original conversation, the director of evaluation was terminated, and the nonprofit lost a twenty-year veteran with deep dedication to the nonprofit.

So, if you choose to embed evaluation into an existing staff role, how can you set the transition up for success?

Be Intentional about Where Evaluation Should Be Integrated

Think about both the department that makes the most sense and the individuals who might have a strong skill set for evaluation. Although the development department is a common place for evaluation to reside, I've seen more success when it's embedded in the program department. Think about the content in **Part Two:** evaluation should be aligned with what the nonprofit and program need to understand better, not what the funders need to know better, and development staff are naturally oriented towards the needs of funders. Remember that it may not be immediately obvious which specific staff member should adopt evaluation—consider a trial rotation period where multiple staff members can see if evaluation resonates with them.

Reallocate Other Responsibilities and Elevate Evaluation

When you add anything new to staff roles, something else has to come off their plates. In addition to making sure that the staff member has the bandwidth to dedicate to evaluation, it is equally critical that evaluation is prioritized as much as other responsibilities. Include it in performance reviews, consider adding it to the position title, and dedicate professional development dollars to building evaluation skills.

Invest in Capacity Building

Evaluation is a specialized skill set that you can't learn completely through a book or a course. Much of evaluation is learned on the job. But it is equally risky to attempt to learn on the job with no support. Find external evaluation experts with experience coaching others. Engage them in the short-term to provide evaluation capacity building for the staff learning evaluation. And in the long-term, be sure that your new evaluation-responsible staff are engaging with the evaluation professional community for ongoing growth and learning.

Be Patient

It takes time for staff, both those who have had evaluation responsibilities added and those who have not, to adjust to role changes. Give the transition time and support it with your best change management techniques.

Hiring a New Internal Evaluator to Join Your Team

There is a classic and vicious cycle in nonprofit evaluation. A nonprofit dabbles in evaluation for a few years, either using existing staff or an external contractor. The staff then hit a point where they or their funder decides it would be a good idea to "up their game" by bringing an evaluator in-house. The staff members, who are not clear on what exactly they are looking for in an internal evaluator, write a unicorn job description including all the possible roles and responsibilities evaluation *might* play. And then they put a $40,000 annual salary on it, because that is the usual starting salary for a coordinator-level position. So they get a pool of applicants with some but not all of the skill sets they listed, and they end up making the selection based on personality rather than the segment of the skills that they need most. And because the position was priced for nonprofit staff, and not evaluation staff, they end up with a recent college graduate with a math background, but no evaluation experience.

The new internal evaluator starts, and falls in love with evaluation, but the supervisory position has no clue what evaluation means and can't provide support or guidance in the field. The new evaluator feels lonely and disconnected as the only evaluator at the nonprofit, and resigns after a year to pursue a different evaluation job with more support. And while the internal evaluator dabbled in helping the nonprofit grow its evaluation capacity, it did not "up their game" because the internal evaluator lacked the evaluation specific skills to make that happen. So the nonprofit starts again at the beginning and repeats the cycle year after year.

It does not have to be this way. Recently, I have begun to work with nonprofits to rethink how they staff internal evaluation roles. One of the first nonprofits we worked with in staffing and recruiting had been in the throes of the vicious internal evaluator mismatch cycle for the past eight years. With the most recent turnover, staff took the time to pause with me and assess what they needed their evaluation function to achieve in the future.

Using an adapted process similar to **Chapters Three** to **Five,** I helped them articulate the most important roles and responsibilities for the internal evaluation role. We thought carefully through the implications of each potential department where evaluation could live. And then we developed a job description that matched the core roles and responsibilities. The internal team lacked experience in evaluation, but I was able to "reality check" what they were seeking against what was possible. I pushed them to prioritize subsets of the evaluation skill sets aligned with what they needed the position to achieve instead of creating a laundry list of equally weighted responsibilities.

We also worked to align the roles and responsibilities with the salary, using evaluation industry benchmarks instead of nonprofit benchmarks. Then we jointly distributed the position and eagerly awaited the applications. To our shock and delight, the quality of the applicant pool was much higher than in previous hiring rounds and more closely aligned with the skill sets the nonprofit needed. In particular, staff sought an evaluator who was able to marry technical skills with facilitation skills to promote learning. Previous hiring rounds had only yielded technical skills, but the majority of new candidates had both.

What's more, the nonprofit received incredible feedback from candidates about the quality of the job description and the clear care that went into crafting the role. In the end, the person hired looks completely different from previous hires, having a PhD and a background in the technical work required. But it's been ten years since the candidate did the technical work, focusing instead on building and managing a technical team. The value added to the nonprofit is in the marriage of technical skills with the ability to build a learning culture.

Setting an Evaluation New Hire Up for Success

So, if you choose to add a new internal evaluation role to your team, how can you set up the new hire for success?

Prioritize a Subset of Evaluation Skills

Evaluators who are good at every nook and cranny of evaluation are few and far between. Some evaluators lean more on the quantitative side and others qualitative. Some evaluators prioritize technical rigor above all else, and others care more about usability and learning. Do not leave these biases to chance. Before crafting the position, decide what orientation is most critical to your nonprofit. Then resist the urge to throw everything else into the job description, too. And don't forget that interpersonal skills, like facilitation and change management skills, are equally important to a good evaluator as research skills.

Be Intentional about Placement on the Organizational Chart

In an ideal world, the evaluation staff should report directly to the executive director. In my experience, this is the only way to truly give evaluation the voice it needs to do its job well, and to make clear the priority the nonprofit puts on evaluation. More often, nonprofits decide to put evaluation in either the programs department or the operations department. There is no solution that works for every nonprofit. Consider the pros and cons of both options and what would work best in your situation. In the programs department, evaluators remain closely aligned with the programs, but sometimes that alignment can get too close and they may resist uncovering negative findings about their boss and close coworkers. In the operations department, evaluators have some distance from the people and services they are evaluating, which can create a greater sense of objectivity but can also create misalignment and tension between the evaluation and the programs.

Use Evaluation Salaries, Not Nonprofit Salaries

Evaluators are on a different pay scale than most other nonprofit staff. There is a higher rate of advanced degrees among evaluators, a more technical skill set, and a smaller supply pool. You are competing against consulting firms and government agencies for evaluation staff, not other nonprofits, so the positions should be salaried accordingly.

Provide Ongoing Support and Connection to the Larger Field

Internal evaluation is a lonely job. Almost everyone on my staff has previously been an internal evaluator and chose to join my team to no longer be the only evaluator in the room. Combat this feeling of isolation by encouraging connections to the larger evaluation field locally, nationally, and virtually.

Contracting with an External Evaluator

The last option for staffing evaluation is to contract with an external evaluator or evaluation firm. Contracting does not mean that you get to relinquish all responsibility for evaluation. The reality of external contracting is that you can never fully outsource evaluation: the nonprofit still needs to contribute to the front-end thinking, as I explained in **Chapter Four,** and the back-end learning, as we discussed in **Chapter Seven.** In addition, there is always going to be a component of the evaluation that requires staff engagement, like distributing survey tools or helping with interview recruitment. The advantage of contracting with an external evaluator is that it allows nonprofits to leverage resources to access a higher level of evaluation expertise than they could afford to hire internally. When contracting with an evaluation team, the nonprofit then has access to multiple evaluation experts, hopefully with complementary skills. The risk with contracting is that evaluation may forever remain peripheral to the nonprofit.

In cases where this works well, the executive director takes care to ensure that the external contractor is still seen as a core element of the nonprofit. One nonprofit that my team and I worked with decided that evaluation was important enough that it should report directly to the nonprofit's executive director. This nonprofit has a twenty-one-person executive team and a $15 million annual budget, and yet the executive director still decided that evaluation was critical enough to handle personally. The executive director took responsibility for maintaining staff engagement throughout the evaluation and integrating the findings into ongoing decision-making. As a result, the evaluation was seen as a critical function of the nonprofit. While not internal to the nonprofit, in many ways, evaluation functioned as an equal partner with programs.

In other cases, management of the evaluation is relegated to a staff member with less authority, or worse, to a committee of staff members. In another nonprofit that my team and I worked with, the development team applied for funding for an evaluation, and then passed the project off to the program team. It quickly became clear that the program staff were not interested in the evaluation at all—let alone having to play an active role in the evaluation. They wanted us to go away and come back in nine months with positive results. No individual staff member on the program team was identified as the main point of contact. Soliciting the staff's input or assistance was like pulling teeth. And when the evaluation was complete, there was no one to take ownership of the report. The end report was reviewed and sent to the funder and never used to inform strategic decisions.

To RFP or Not to RFP?

If you decide to go the direction of contracting with an external evaluator, the natural question that follows is how to find an external evaluator. And just the approach you take to finding an evaluator can have serious implications for the quality of your experience with that evaluation. The two common approaches are to release a formal competitive Request for Proposals (RFP) or to informally solicit proposals from a smaller group of evaluators. I know that some nonprofits have competitive RFP processes written into their governance bylaws. If that is the case, feel free to skip forward to the next section.

RFPs are more common in evaluation contracting than other types of nonprofit services. Did you RFP for your last strategic planning process? Your grant writer? How about your auditor? There is a perception that nonprofits should use a competitive bid RFP process for evaluators, even if they do not for other services, to make sure the evaluator is "objective." Objectivity is important, but that comes from the training and ethics of the evaluation team, not from the selection process. In fact, the RFP process itself can lead to a *less* objective evaluator. Let's explore this further:

Two Counterproductive Factors with the RFP Process

There are two factors that can make the RFP process counterproductive to finding a high-quality, objective evaluator. The first factor falls into the contracting nonprofit's purview and the second factor falls into the consulting evaluator's realm.

The Nonprofit's Purview

Perhaps you work for a nonprofit that needs to hire an evaluation consultant because you don't have the expertise to conduct the evaluation yourself. Many nonprofits proceed with an RFP process. In most RFPs, I commonly see very specific scope of work for what the nonprofit is requesting: it has already set the focus of the evaluation and seems to be looking for someone to carry out that approach.

The nonprofit gets a number of responses to the RFP. Some are tailored carefully to the needs stipulated in the RFP, while others provide a new approach based on a different perspective.

For example, the RFP may have focused on learning about the implementation of the program and participant reactions to the program structure. But one evaluation firm has expertise in educational outcomes and rigorous experimental designs, so it proposes randomizing participants into the program or a control group and testing educational outcomes. Because the hiring nonprofit did not quite know what was needed when writing the RFP, it finds something shiny in the new perspectives and decides that was what they wanted! The board would love to see educational outcomes!

But the program is nascent, in its second year, and the program staff needed information about program implementation before outcome data would be useful. Suddenly, the nonprofit has contracted with an evaluator with a very particular approach to evaluation instead an evaluator that is responsive to the nonprofit's needs. Sounds really objective, right? The nonprofit continues with the evaluation contractor focused on educational outcomes and doesn't find the results they hoped for. The staff are frustrated and say, "Of course we didn't change educational outcomes, we are still working out the kinks of program delivery," and the next time the nonprofit wants to do an evaluation, the program team will not cooperate. I see the pattern again and again, with nonprofits using an RFP, that then end up with an evaluation focused in an entirely different direction than the RFP stipulated.

The Contracted Evaluator

The second counterproductive factor of the RFP process is related to the contracting evaluator: the skills that make for a good RFP response are not the same as the skills that make for a good evaluation partner. As we've discussed throughout this book, the best evaluations are oriented to helping a nonprofit learn and grow with the insights gained through evaluation. RFP responses are terrible at revealing whether a contractor would be a good partner in the learning process. The most important criteria for an effective learning process with an external partner are trust, a strong working relationship, and an ability to handle complexity and uncertainty.

The best RFP responses highlight expertise and suggest certainty and clarity where there is none. In fact, the nonprofits that are best at RFP responses are those that have specific business development teams to respond to these RFPs. So, the staff member who wrote the RFP response is rarely the staff member with whom you will be working directly. And this downside doesn't account for the effects of artificial restrictions placed on RFPs, like formatting and page limit, which further restrict the quality of responses and often unfairly benefit simpler designs regardless of the complexity of your project. The unfortunate reality is that a majority of the best evaluators I know *don't respond to RFPs* because the structure of the selection process does not allow them to highlight what makes them great evaluators.

The alternative to an RFP process is to informally solicit project proposals from a few pre-vetted evaluation partners. Seek recommendations from funders with whom you have a strong relationship and other nonprofits that have invested heavily in evaluation. Most regions have a local affiliate of the American Evaluation Association; look it up and find out which consultants are active in the local evaluation community. The American Evaluation Association also has a "Find an Evaluator" feature where you can look up consultants in your area. I recommend that hiring nonprofits speak with at least three potential evaluation contractors. Your first goal is to assess whether the contractor would be a good partner in your learning journey. Only then should you double check technical skills, looking both at methodological and research qualifications as well as facilitation and change management chops.

After you've had that initial meeting, you should absolutely request proposals. In my experience as both a funder who managed evaluation contracts and as an evaluation contractor, the solicited-proposals approach is more productive to finding a good evaluation partner for a learning-oriented, client-centric evaluation. Once you've identified a contractor whose perspective and approach align with your needs, together you can craft an evaluation that targets the things you need to learn most.

Some Suggestions for Using the RFP Process

If you decided to go through an RFP process despite the downsides outlined above, there are few small ways that you can make it more likely to succeed:

Set a Reasonable Budget

It is extremely common for a nonprofit's evaluation wish list to outgrow the budget available. The rule of thumb is that evaluation should be 10 percent of the program budget—not the grant budget—or $5,000, whichever is larger. So what can you get for that budget? It's always a good idea to "reality check" your budget and your wish list with a trained evaluator before getting started with the project.

Strategically Identify a Single Staff Member

My worst work experiences are those where the nonprofit failed to identify a single point person, and those where my main point person has limited authority within the nonprofit. It is critical to have one staff member to act as a bridge between the nonprofit and the contractor. And, it is equally critical that the point person has some authority within the nonprofit. A good practice to keep in mind is that the staff member managing the evaluation contract should be at the same seniority level as the most senior program staff person.

Expect to Assist With Execution

There are elements of the evaluation that are always going to be more effective when coming from the program staff. Some examples include distributing a survey or recruiting for interviews. You've got the list of names already, and the recipients are more likely to respond if they recognize the sender. Another example is hosting in-person data collection. Your location is familiar and safe, while ours is not. Don't be surprised when these "asks" come from your evaluation contractor, and set the expectation of cooperation with your staff in advance.

Take Ownership Over Direction and Reflection

You can never fully outsource the strategic aspects of evaluation. You and your team should play the leading role in setting the key evaluation questions and evaluation direction with your contractor in a support and facilitation role. Then the roles reverse for executing the evaluation, with the contractor leading the process and your team supporting the contractor. The roles reverse again when the results are in, with the internal staff back in the lead role to reflect and learn. The only way for evaluation to blend into the fabric of a nonprofit is by having staff, particularly leadership, engaged in interpreting the results and determining the strategic implications of the work.

When Not to Evaluate

I'm sneaking in one last option for staffing evaluation: don't staff it. Not every nonprofit needs to invest additional resources into evaluation. In fact, there are two primary reasons you might correctly choose not to integrate more evaluation work into your nonprofit.

First, do not invest in evaluation if there are no circumstances under which you will change your programming based on the evaluation findings. The purpose of evaluation is to learn, grow, and continue to improve programs—and by extension the impact on our communities. If your nonprofit is dedicated to the specific way you do things to such an extent that no change is possible, then it is not worth the resources to find out what you should be doing differently. I very much doubt that this describes you, because you wouldn't be reading this book if you weren't interested in learning and growing!

Second, do not invest in evaluation if you do not have the resources to do it well. If you saw the comments in previous sections about evaluation salaries instead of nonprofit salaries, or shooting for 10 percent of your program budget and balked, it may not be the right time for you to pursue evaluation. I have found that mediocre evaluations are worse for the nonprofit than no evaluation. If you half-heartedly pursue evaluation, you may end up basing important programmatic and nonprofit decisions on faulty information under the guise of objectivity. Do not make a major push toward evaluation until you have budget to do so. And if your funders are pressuring you to do so, share **Chapter Twelve** of this book with them and advocate for them to provide an adequate evaluation budget as part of their funding.

Communicating About Evaluation

Before and after making a decision about how to staff evaluation, you will still play a role in communicating internally and externally about evaluation. Evaluation is not a "set it and forget it" activity: for evaluation to live up to its potential, it requires ongoing executive support. I close this chapter with a few quick tips on how to communicate about evaluation with internal and external audiences from a leadership position.

Communicating Internally

As the executive director, your most important role in supporting evaluation internally is two-fold: building a culture of evaluation by elevating its importance, and building the capacity of your team to engage productively with evaluation. There is no magic bullet for either of these areas. The key is repetition of the key concepts in **Part Two** of this book. Some ideas of ongoing messaging include:

Evaluation as a Learning Process

Continue to frame evaluation as a tool for ongoing learning and strategic improvement, not accountability and punitive measures. Especially in the early days of implementing a learning-oriented evaluation approach, any slippage back into an accountability mindset can set back the process. As the leader of the nonprofit, it falls on you to call out and correct the accountability lens when it creeps in. Hold the mantle for learning and help your staff adjust to that new way of doing things.

Evaluation as a Core Function

It is easy for evaluation to slide to the back burner behind day-to-day program implementation and keeping the lights on. Emphasize the importance of evaluation and its primacy to nonprofits' ability to serve the mission.

Evaluation Is About People, Not Data

While you need some support on the technical side, the rest of your staff need not be technical experts to engage with evaluation. Refer to the "Staffing Evaluation" section above. Continually remind staff that evaluation is not about math and numbers, but about the people you serve, which the numbers represent. And make sure that your technical evaluation staff remember that principle as well, engaging the team in evaluation and using language they can access.

Because Evaluation Is a Learning Process

If evaluation is a learning process, then it makes sense that we continue to learn how to do evaluation. The goal is no longer a "perfect" evaluation, but an evaluation from which we learn. Support your team's ongoing learning and growth around evaluation. Seek out professional development resources and encourage the team to include evaluation-related goals in performance reviews.

Communicating Externally

Beyond your direct staff, you also play a critical role in supporting evaluation at the board level and externally with funders and partners. In these spaces, it's helpful to remember that taking a learning-orientation to evaluation as presented throughout this book is not universal. The evaluation approach you are building is leading a change and moving against the status quo. As a result, the most important external communication role you play is to lead that change by educating those outside the nonprofit. The language from **Part One** can inform the way you present evaluation externally. Some specific ideas of what to share include:

Focus on the "Why"

When talking evaluation with your board and beyond, emphasize why evaluation is important to the nonprofit, *not* what you are going to evaluate. Remember, the evaluation purpose statement we introduced in **Chapter Three** sets the big picture reasons for evaluating and should last for three to five years. The specific focus on key evaluation questions and evaluation methods might change every year. Share with your external stakeholders why you've decided to invest in learning-focused evaluation. Give some examples of how the new approach has helped engage your staff and improve your programming.

Educate on Evaluation as Learning

There are many funders, donors, and board members who retain accountability-focused perspectives on evaluation. The first step is to educate them about alternative ways to think about evaluation. Most of the time, their focus on accountability is because that's all they've been exposed to. Share this book with them and have a conversation about the differences between their thinking and yours. Then, push back on accountability-focused evaluation in grant requirements and board requests. As I shared in **Chapter Ten,** funders want to know you are a strategic nonprofit using their resources to make a difference in the community. Learning-focused evaluation can show that just as well, if not better than their accountability-focused reports. I have never in my career seen a funder say "no" when a nonprofit presents an alternative evaluation report that is tailored to its work and has informed tangible improvements to its programming. **Chapter Eleven** is also a useful read for executive directors and speaks specifically on how to have conversations about evaluation at the board level.

Integrate Evaluation Messages Everywhere

The nonprofits I've seen that have truly integrated evaluation have integrated it into their external messages as well. For example, one nonprofit opens its fundraising luncheon with a discussion about why staff members invest in evaluation and what they've learned over the past year. Another has reformatted sections of its annual report to align with key evaluation questions. And another regularly posts blog updates on the evaluation process and results. Consider where in your external-facing communications it would make sense to infuse your messaging with evaluation.

At this point, I hope you've found a few useful tips to strengthen how you, as the leader of the nonprofit, engage in evaluation. What one thing can you take away and immediately implement in your nonprofit? Hand this book and your evaluation commitment off to the communications team at your nonprofit.

Chapter Nine

The Communications Team

In this chapter, we focus on how evaluation can help the communications team and how the communications team can help evaluation. We explore how to evaluate events and conferences, reports and publications, and social media. Then we dive into how the communications team can support evaluation by messaging evaluation as learning, focusing on contribution rather than attribution, and closing the feedback loop with beneficiaries.

As a member of a nonprofit communications team, you play a dual role: you mobilize communication vehicles to achieve your nonprofit's mission *and* you use those vehicles to promote your nonprofit's progress towards its mission. Evaluation intersects with both these roles: first, you can use evaluation to understand whether and how your communication efforts are moving the needle on your nonprofit mission. Second, you can translate and disseminate evaluation findings to communicate the success and impact of your nonprofit. In this chapter, I share some easy-to-implement tips and tricks to make the communications team masters of using and sharing evaluation. But first, let's begin with an interesting story about Businesses Unite.

Businesses Unite

Meet Brandon, the Vice President of Communications and Marketing for a five-thousand-member membership association, Businesses Unite. Brandon had previously worked for an advertising agency with a large budget to support sophisticated communications efforts. But at Businesses Unite, he had to do more with less: instead of a communicating a singular message to a singular target with a large budget to do so, Brandon was charged with communicating about the association's many programs to members, potential members, and policymakers with a budget less than 10 percent of what he was used to.

After three years of trying everything he could think of to serve all of the core messages to all the target audiences well, he was ready to throw in the towel. Internally, program directors said their attendance wasn't what it should be because Brandon's team was not communicating their events enough. Externally, members said that they received too many communications from Businesses Unite, and unsubscribe requests to the email list were skyrocketing. Between a rock and a hard place, Brandon looked to the annual membership survey for help. Could members help Businesses Unite prioritize messaging to the areas that they cared most about?

Brandon sat down with Anita, Businesses Unite's Chief Operating Officer, to discuss that year's membership survey. The nonprofit had always done the membership survey in-house and, looking back, it was clear that the survey did not generate much useful information to inform a communications strategy. Then Anita remembered meeting me at one of Businesses Unite's events and reached out to see if I could help. I worked with the full executive team to articulate key evaluation questions for the membership survey, using the process in **Chapter Four.** And to Brandon's delight, one of the key evaluation questions that rose to the top was: what are the most and least effective communication vehicles for Businesses Unite to communicate its value to members?

With that question and others in mind, I transitioned the membership survey to a "membership feedback process" including both a survey and a series of follow-up focus groups. The survey confirmed what Brandon already knew: members were not taking advantage of the many programs Businesses Unite made available. And the large number of emails they already received from the nonprofit irritated members, to the point of reducing the perceived value of their membership. But like previous years, the survey did not uncover useful suggestions to improve and prioritize messaging. Because as we learned in **Chapter Five,** a survey was not and had never been the right instrument to answer that question.

The focus groups were another story. My team, in collaboration with Brandon and Anita, developed an interactive focus group approach. The first step asked the group to develop a list of what participants would like to hear about from Businesses Unite. What did they care about? What did they want information about? This step revealed many of the same things we knew from the survey: that people had "favorite" events, and generally they wanted to network and learn. Not much new information here. But the second step dug deeply into why the group wanted to know about each group of items. What about the content mattered to them?

Here's Where The Magic Started

By pushing the group to articulate why they wanted to hear about certain events, we began to gain a more generalizable understanding of what members valued in Businesses Unite's communications. Instead of sending out an email about each networking event because members like networking, we started to see the components and goals of networking that resonated with members. And in the last step, we asked the group to prioritize only three areas to receive communications about. Brandon expected the usual pattern to emerge: members want such different things from Businesses Unite that the priorities would not converge. But the opposite happened. After articulating the why behind the content requests, a clear set of priority areas emerged.

By using evaluation intentionally, with a clear focus on the things he needed to know most and engaging the right methods to answer those key questions, Brandon finally had the information he was so desperate for. With the findings from the focus groups, Brandon crafted a new communication strategy. He was able to push back on program directors' request for more communication with clear feedback from members. He was able to reduce the number of email communications while increasing the alignment of communications with member feedback. And slowly but surely, the complaints about email volume decreased, while perceived value increased.

Brandon's role in the evaluation didn't stop there. He also embraced the communications team's ability to support evaluation by closing the feedback loop with members. After the membership feedback process, he crafted an "informative thank-you note" using the strategies in **Chapter Seven** and shared it with the members. In this way, it was clear to members that their feedback was valued and used, and that Businesses Unite was truly a member-driven membership association.

In this example, we see an in-depth case study of how evaluation can be used in service of the communications team and how the communications team can be in service of the evaluation. Throughout the rest of this chapter, I offer some of the key lessons that helped Brandon maximize the benefit of evaluation to Businesses Unite. First, we focus on evaluation in service

of the communications team. Then we conclude with how communication
can support evaluation.

Evaluation in Service of Communications

Nonprofit communication work is often a program strategy, especially
for advocacy nonprofits. You use events to educate your target audience
about an issue. You deliver publications and reports to call readers to
action. You apply social media to generate a conversation between your
audience members and build a sense of community. All three of these are
programming strategies that can and should be evaluated. And, I don't
mean by reporting the lowest common denominator of communication
work: number of people who attended an event and the number of reports
you passed out. I mean evaluation that helps you learn about what you are
doing well and what you could improve in the future.

The first steps in evaluating communication vehicles are the same as any
other type of programming: gain clarity on what it is you are evaluating
and what you are hoping to achieve, as we emphasized in **Chapter
Three.** Articulate what you need to learn from the evaluation like we
discussed in **Chapter Four.** Use those questions to determine the research
methods you are using as seen in **Chapter Five.** The differences come up
in the methods that are available to you and in how you might execute
an evaluation in a communications context. Let's take a look at special
evaluation considerations for three key communication vehicles: events
and conferences, publications and reports, and social media.

Events and Conferences

Let's say you host an event to educate your audience and promote your
nonprofit's work. I bet you know what comes next. You say, "A post-event
survey, of course!" Please, no! Please, no more post-event surveys asking
how I liked the food and whether I was satisfied with the speakers!

Post-event surveys have become the "must-do" for "strategic nonprofits."
But now think about the last post-event survey you used. How much new
information did you learn? I bet you heard things like, "The ballroom
was too cold" and "The chicken for lunch was dry." Okay, well, you are a
nonprofit with limited resources and that was the event space you could
afford. And you've already booked it for next year, so too bad your guests
didn't like the temperature and the food. That kind of feedback is not going
change what you do.

You say, "Okay, but I also ask questions about the quality of the speakers." Does a one-to-five rating of a specific speaker change what you do? Are you really going to use that speaker again? If the rating is really high or really low, do you know why? Without understanding what about the speaker was received well or poorly, speaker ratings are just as worthless as temperature or food feedback.

So, how might you evaluate an event in a way that generates information that actually helps your nonprofit communications team plan for future events?

My number-one tip is to reconsider whether you actually need a post-event survey. Post-event surveys have become so ubiquitous that people have stopped paying attention to them. Response rates drop because you distribute so many post-event surveys, which ask seemingly irrelevant questions, and your feedback on the food never improves the food! So why send a post-event survey at all? The answer most nonprofits give is that they need feedback. But why not consider alternative modes of feedback?

My favorite event evaluation strategy is to use "point-of-contact" evaluations. These are short and sweet data collection opportunities at the time when people are in front of you. Instead of sending a post-event survey, ask attendees your questions before they leave the event. I don't mean paper surveys that you have to manually enter to get the same worthless data as your electronic post-event survey. I mean using a mix of creative, real-time feedback opportunities, like:

If you want to know...	Try...
How attendees are engaging	Structured Observation: Use a tailored checklist to observe how attendees interact with components of the event and each other. How many people attend a session and how many leave midway through? How many questions are asked? Are attendees participating or texting? Observation captures information about the attendees' engagement during the event in an unobtrusive way that complements feedback from attendees.

How attendees are reacting	"Color Scripting":[10] Throughout the event, ask attendees to fill out cards with one question: How do you feel right now about what you are learning? Then back in your office, group the cards by emotion, such as overwhelmed, excited, and processing. Then examine how the dominant emotion changes over time. A good event has a planned ebb and flow of emotion, and this approach helps map whether attendees experienced the event in the way you hoped they would. This method works best for a full day or longer event.
What attendees are learning (individual)	Mini-Interviews: Audio- or video-record attendees answering a single interview question as they move through the event. What is the most interesting thing they learned? What is their most important takeaway? Different questions may be positioned in different locations throughout the event to understand attendee perspectives and reactions to different components or sessions.
What attendees are learning (collective)	Learning Wall: Prompt attendees to post one piece of information or strategy that they learned on a wall display. Subsequent attendees can add a new learning, reemphasize an old one with a sticker, or add additional detail to something already posted, creating an interactive assessment tool that can inform the evaluation of the event content and create an opportunity for attendees to share with each other.
What action attendees will take afterward (individual and collective)	Commitment Cards: Ask attendees to fill out cards stating one action they plan to take as a result of the event. Sort the completed cards throughout the event and hang them by theme on a public display so all event attendees can see the anticipated changes as a result of the collective action.

10 Tackett, Wendy. "Color Scripting: Adapting A Disney-Pixar Tool For Use In Evaluation." Speech, Conference, Washington D.C., 2017.

	Suggestion Wheel: Ask attendees what they would like to see more of, less of, stopped, started, and continued via a public display poster. Each attendee adds a sticky note or two or adds a vote to an existing comment. This gathers immediate and direct feedback on what was most useful about the event and what aspects could be improved.
What about the event should you replicate or change	

Tips to Promote Participation

Admittedly, attendees will be unfamiliar with some of these approaches to evaluating an event. To help acclimate them to these strategies I've mentioned in the table, consider these ideas:

◆ Promise that you won't send out a post-event survey and keep your promise.

◆ Use energetic staff and volunteers to oversee the point of contact evaluations. My team has gone as far as using fun things like brightly colored branded t-shirts and waist packs to identify the evaluation team and create a conversation starter.

◆ Create a passport program, where attendees win prizes or are entered into drawings based on how many point-of-contact evaluations they participate in.

◆ Profusely thank attendees for participating during and after the event. In that email you formerly used for the post-event survey, why not share some of the things you learned from the point-of-contact evaluations and how you plan to change your approach accordingly? See **Chapter Seven** for more details about informative thank-you notes.

Reports and Publications: The Evaluation Dilemma

Do you know what happens with your report or publication after you post it on your website? I rarely see evaluation of written communication materials go beyond number of copies distributed, which definitely does not tell you whether that material made a difference. And it's hard because people get fed so many publications that it's nearly impossible to know what piece of information actually impacted a change in thinking or behavior. Connecting a change in thinking or behavior to your report instead of any of the other influences in the audience's life is tricky. So, you have two choices:

It Is Okay to Not Evaluate a Report or Publication

Yes, I just said it's okay not to evaluate. In **Chapter Ten,** we'll talk about how you could spend your entire nonprofit budget on evaluation and still not have a perfectly rigorous evaluation of every program. You have to make some tough decisions about what to evaluate and what not to evaluate within the context of the resources you have available. And often reports and publications are the first thing to get cut from the "things we should evaluate" list. You can simply produce publications because it feels like the right thing to do, monitor the number of downloads and call it a day. But if you take this approach, don't call the number of downloads an evaluation of the publication. You have no idea who is downloading it, for what purpose and whether it is influencing behavior. Call it what it is. Justify the report based on the fact that the nonprofit values distributing information. Don't hide behind fake evaluation.

Decide on What You Really Hope to Find

Alternatively, you can commit to evaluating what matters about a publication and accept that it will take more money and time than past publication evaluations have. In this case, narrow in on what you really hope the report will achieve and invest the resources into evaluating whether that outcome can happen. Notice that I did not say "does" happen, I said "can" happen. For most nonprofits in the real world, evaluating how many people changed their minds because of a publication is not an answerable question, as I explained in **Chapter Four.** Again, there are many competing inputs and a lot of contextual factors you have no control over. So, we reframe it as an answerable question: for a small group of people, *can* this publication change minds? My team and I have used two approaches successfully in evaluating publications and reports: user testing by interviews and following the publication's distribution path.

User Testing

In user testing, we sit down with individuals in the target audience for a publication before it's publicly released and ask them questions about the publication. We start with some basic questions about their perceptions of an issue and sometimes ask about what other sources they consult for information on the topic. Then we share the resource with them and give them time to read and review it. If your publication is long, this is going to be a long interview! We ask the test participants to narrate out loud as they navigate the report: what catches their eye? What information did they already know and what is new? What doesn't make sense? And if accessibility or navigability is a top question, we'll ask prompting questions to have them look for specific pieces. At the end, we will ask some wrap-up questions about what they learned and what, if anything, changed their thinking. We'll also ask for recommendations for improvement and who they think might find the publication useful.

We never use a survey for user testing. Sometimes nonprofits want to use a pre- or post-test to measure whether perceptions change before and after reading a publication. We strongly discourage you from wasting your evaluation dollars on this approach. It's hard to change perceptions. One publication is just not strong enough. Again, what you are trying to capture in user testing is not *whether* the publication changes minds, but *can* the publication change minds. Understanding the change mechanism is the most important piece, and as you learned in **Chapter Five,** qualitative approaches are best suited for revealing the mechanism.

Following a Distribution Path

The second evaluation approach my team has used is less focused on the publication itself and more focused on how the publication reaches your target audience. Using this approach, you create a miniature interview guide, with no more than five questions in ten minutes. You start by asking how participants found the publication. Then you ask a few critical questions about their reactions to or with the publication. And then the last question is always what they did with the publication: did they share it with a colleague, and if so, who? Did they share it on social media? Post it on their nonprofit's website? The first people you ask these questions of should be people closest to your nonprofit, who you know saw the publication. Start with about five people.

Then use "snowball sampling": the next people you ask are the people who your current group of interviewees identified in the final question. Let the people who used your publication help you find other people who read your publication. And stop when you aren't hearing anything new or when you run out of time. In this way, you can slowly build out a spider web following a small subset of the people who interacted with your publication, and understand the ways that people found the publication and what they did with it.

Social Media Metrics: Helpful or Not?

While we have very little data about the influence of a publication, we have tons of data about the influence of social media content! Just open up Facebook Insights, or one of many social media platforms, and you'll be flooded with hundreds of numbers to tell you just how big an impact your social media work has, right? Look a little closer and you'll begin to realize that most of those numbers are just noise. What do you learn from knowing that five thousand people watched your video for ten seconds? What is the value of reporting both the comments, shares, and reactions on a post and the combined comments, shares, and reactions?

The unfortunate truth is that too many nonprofit communications teams pull the Facebook Insights data and plop them into a report without even thinking about what they mean. They are satisfied with reporting the huge number of impressions their content made or that they are meeting their benchmark engagement rates without ever thinking about what the data mean and how they can help inform and improve communication practices. Because Facebook did the work for us, right? It picks the best metrics! Unfortunately, that's not Facebook's job. Facebook is motivated to make you feel good by sharing a ton of data with you so that at least one aspect will support your assumptions that your content is working, and to keep you using Facebook as an "effective" communication tool. It's your job not to be fooled and to dig deeper into what social media data is telling you, as well as what you can learn to improve your work.

In the case of social media content, you have the opposite problem you did with publications: the question isn't how do you get data, but how do you find meaning in too much data? The good news here is that my team and I have already done that legwork for you. Having conducted an evaluation on an entirely social media-based program, we have become accidental experts in evaluating social media content. Through years of trial and error, I have narrowed down the most important analytics to look at depending on—you guessed it—what you are trying to learn. Before sharing those specifics with you, here are four guiding principles to keep in mind when evaluating social media content:

Just Because It's There Does Not Mean It's Useful

At the time this book was written, Facebook insights provided forty-two data points *about each and every Facebook post*. If you post one thousand pieces of content in a year, that means 42,000 data points to dig through.

Some of that, yes, is useful. But, it depends heavily on Facebook's reporting of impressions and engagements, where much of the data is duplicative or irrelevant. For example, Facebook duplicates facts like number of people and number of clicks while giving you unnecessary metrics like three-second views. If you make one change to how you evaluate social media as a result of this book, look at *less* data. Use the cheat sheet below to narrow in on what actually helps you understand your impact on social media.

The "Right" Metrics Depend on the Goal

When my team started our social media evaluation work, our partners monitored engagement rates for each and every post and compared engagement rates across all posts. But we quickly learned the engagement rates were highest for warm fuzzy motivational content and lowest for content that challenged the audience to think deeply. Does a low engagement rate mean that the challenging content is not working, and we should only share warm fuzzies? No. It just means our metrics were wrong and we shouldn't be comparing apples to oranges. That's why the cheat sheet is broken up by goals.

Metrics Can't Tell You Everything

Analytics data rarely tell you *why* something is happening. You might know that a particular post had an unusually high number of shares, but why was the content so shareable? For this, you need to get beyond analytics. My team uses Facebook comments to understand what people are saying about why certain posts resonate so strongly with them. We also have a group of audience members who we engage with offline to understand at a deeper level why certain content does or does not resonate, much like the user testing process we outlined in the publication evaluation section above. And, we also rely heavily on our content expert partners, who spend each and every day engaged with our audience members. When we see something unexpected in the data, our partners often have a key piece of contextual detail to make sense of it.

Sometimes, the Data is Just Messy

This stuff is not clean and easy and straightforward, despite how the nice graphs on Facebook Insights make it look. Sometimes there are things in the data we just can't explain. Sometimes Facebook changes its algorithm overnight. Keep in mind realistic expectations about what you can and cannot learn from social media.

Social Media Metrics Cheat Sheet: Use these metrics (and only these metrics) to evaluate your social media content

Goal	Facebook	Twitter	Instagram	Email
Generate conversation	# of comments (how many are replies?)	# of replies	Comments	*Email is not the right platform for this goal*
Build awareness	Engagement rate Reach	Engagement rate Impressions	Engagement rate Impressions Saves	Open rate Click-through rate
Grow a network	Reach # of new page follows # of unfollows	Impressions # of new page follows # of unfollows	Impressions # of new page follows # of unfollows	# of forwards & new sign-ups # of unsubscribes
Direct traffic to your website	# of link clicks (Unique users)	# of link clicks	*Instagram is not the right platform for this goal*	Click-through rate
Gain insights on audience behavior	# of comments Clicks Disaggregated reactions	# of replies # of hashtag clicks	# of likes # of saves	*Email is not the right platform for this goal*

How Communication Supports Evaluation

The communications team plays a unique role in communicating about evaluation to the outside world. When you have a good understanding of what evaluation outcomes say about your programs, it can be a powerful tool to communicate the value of your nonprofit. But evaluation rarely produces the sound-bite highlights all communicators dream about, so how do you bridge that gap? Here are three tips to help evaluation and communication become friends.

Evaluation as Learning: An Essential Perspective

First and foremost, frame evaluation in the same way you've learned to see it throughout this book: as a learning process, not an accountability tool. If your nonprofit is asking key evaluation questions that matter, sometimes the evaluation will be positive and sometimes it will suggest areas for improvement. If you position the evaluation as a tool to identify whether or not the nonprofit is doing what it promises, then half the time you'll be left in a pickle about how to share data that doesn't support the message of nonprofit effectiveness.

Instead, when you position evaluation as a tool to help learn and continually improve the nonprofit and its programs, then all evaluation is positive: whether the results support the nonprofit's effectiveness or not, it is an opportunity for learning and growth. Talk about how the *process of* evaluation helps the nonprofit be more effective, not just about how the *results of* evaluation show that the nonprofit is effective.

I know this is easier said than done. It starts with the program team and leadership making an authentic commitment to using evaluation as a learning tool. The communication strategy then follows. You can't communicate about learning if the nonprofit is using evaluation as an accountability check. So, your first job is to support the rest of the nonprofit in arriving at the conclusion that evaluation is learning. In my experience, assurances from the communication and development departments that they can in fact message evaluation as learning goes a long way to increase comfort levels with bucking the status quo.

Embrace Contribution: A More Accurate Communications Position

One of the biggest conflicts between communication and evaluation is how firmly each group feels comfortable phrasing a program's impact. Communicators want to use definitive and causal language about program effects: "*Because of the program*, students improved their literacy skills," "As a result of the program..." "The program produced..." Evaluators push back and say, "We did not do an experiment. We cannot know for sure that students would not have improved their literacy skills anyway, so we cannot say that." Instead, evaluators want to say, "Students improved their literacy skills *during their time in the program*," or simply, "Students improved their literacy skills."

Evaluators focus on the *contribution* that the program made to an impact rather than trying to *attribute* the full impact to the program. I know the communications version is a stronger message and more clearly written. *But unless you have a good understanding of what would happen without the program, the "counterfactual" in research-speak, the communications version is fundamentally inaccurate.*

From a technical perspective, you need an experiment or close to it to justify a causal statement. There are a few ways to get to data that supports a causal statement, but that's beyond the scope of this book. And very few of the nonprofits I interact with are ready for this level of evaluation: it requires a tremendous dedication of resources, both financial and human, and requires a mature program with a consistently implemented program model. Even the lowest cost causal evaluations cost hundreds of thousands of dollars. I recommend this type of evaluation only after years of evaluation, leading up to a probable expectation that the investment will produce strong results.

So, if you really want to make direct causal claims about your program, start with evaluation that makes sense for the maturity of your program and

Overstating: It's Not Worth the Risk

Not everyone in your audience will care or notice if you overstate the direct impact of your programs. But for those who do, it calls into question the accuracy of everything else you say. To me, the credibility of the nonprofit is not worth the risk. Most audiences are sophisticated enough to understand that you are working in a complicated social context with lots of competing inputs that both support and negate the impact you are trying to achieve. In my experience, when you frame the program as contributing to an impact without fully attributing the impact to the program alone, the audience views the program positively anyway. You get the same result without the risk.

the key evaluation questions you've selected. Support evaluation efforts internally and gradually work your way toward having the strongest types of evidence. But keep in mind that it will take years, not months, to get there.

Closing the Feedback Loop

There is a movement throughout the nonprofit field to be more transparent about our work—about how much the work actually costs, particularly in overhead, about how hard the work is, about the funder or grantee relationship, and about collaboration and competition. And that push for transparency is extending to evaluation. There are more and more calls for nonprofits to share their evaluation results, in the same way they share their 990s. I hope you will consider joining this movement.

Now, I don't mean a GuideStar-style summary of impact comparing the same metrics across different programs. As you've gathered from the rest of this book, I take issue with the idea of comparing the same measures of success across different programs. That's evaluation as an accountability tool and has no place in a world of evaluation as a learning process. Each nonprofit's key evaluation questions should mirror its stage of maturity and what it needs to learn most about its programs. Each nonprofit's evaluation should look different.

Instead, I advocate for publicly disseminating your evaluation reports, or at least a summary of them. Share your evaluation and your learning with your beneficiaries, your partners, your funders, and the broader community. You can find detailed advice on how to share evaluation results effectively in **Chapter Seven.**

At this point, I hope you've found a few useful tips to strengthen how your communications team uses evaluation. What one thing can you take away and immediately implement in your nonprofit? Hand this book and your evaluation commitment off to the development team in your nonprofit.

Chapter Ten

The Development Team

In this chapter, I present some of the main lessons that help development staff use evaluation to their advantage, like A/B testing and donor surveys. But first, we spend a little time talking about how to evaluate your own development efforts. Then, we go through three arenas where program evaluation and development intersect: writing the evaluation section of grant applications, presenting evaluation results on grant reports, and having conversations about evaluation with individual, foundation, and corporate donors.

You pursued development work to help a nonprofit you love keep the lights on and deliver programming to change the world. Your skill is in building relationships and communicating with individuals and nonprofits about why the nonprofit you love is amazing and why they, too, should support it. Everything is going well—you are doing a great job of securing funds for your nonprofit. All of a sudden, you start to see questions on your grant applications like, "What are the measurable outcomes your nonprofit is expecting to achieve?" and hear questions from donors such as, "How will I know my dollars are making a difference?"

Ugh. Evaluation has thrown a wrench in your approach. But it doesn't have to be all bad. With a few tweaks to how you think about, talk about, and use evaluation, the suggestions here can transform evaluation from a thorn in your side to a powerful tool that sets you apart from all other funding requests. I'd like to introduce an organization called Books for All that helps us examine these tools more closely. Let's meet Tori.

Books for All

Tori is a development officer who is focused on foundation relations for Books for All, a literacy promotion nonprofit with a $5 million budget. The increased focus on evaluation among funders came as a surprise to Tori: foundations that had supported and trusted the nonprofit for years suddenly wanted more "objective proof" that the program was improving children's reading scores. It felt like the rug had been pulled out from under her. And no matter how many times she tried her usual tactics of sharing success stories, taking funders on site visits, or giving them an inside look at the sophisticated back-end program tracking system, the funders still kept asking for evaluation.

So, Tori went to her colleague Deon, the program director, to ask for evaluation data. Deon pulled out a report Books for All had commissioned annually for the past four years, but never read. Together they sat down to read through the results. To their dismay, neither Deon nor Tori could get the information they needed out of these reports. *Well, that just won't do,* they decided, and together they went on a quest to improve their evaluation practices, both for the development team *and* the program team.

Deon reached out to me in the middle of a programming year, seeking a replacement for their current evaluation vendor. Deon expressed the need for an evaluation partner who could help them think through what kind of evaluation would meet the nonprofit's needs, but also be compelling to funders. We started working together using the process outlined in **Part Two** of this book. In our first meeting, we talked about mapping the program and articulating questions to guide the evaluation.

Later, when I came back with an evaluation plan and news that we'd have to quadruple their very low evaluation budget to get the information they wanted, Tori was the first one on board and spent the next several months securing funding for the increase. She worked directly with me to craft language about Books for All's shifting evaluation approach that would most resonate with funders. And when the evaluation was complete, Tori dove the deepest into the findings, reading the report carefully, asking a ton of excellent questions, and thinking through how to present this information back to the funders.

In this evaluation, the program team ended the year with information they could use to tweak programming. And Tori also got what she needed out of it. Armed with an increased understanding of evaluation and a specific example of how it can help Books for All, Tori and her team had the most successful foundation funding year in their history, supporting both the program and continued evaluation efforts.

Evaluating Development

Many of the face-to-face events and online or print communications mobilized for development work can use the same evaluation strategies I recommend for the communications team in **Chapter Nine,** so consider starting your evaluation journey there. However, there are evaluation opportunities specific to the development team. In this section, we focus on two of them: direct mail or email fundraising, and donor surveys.

Does Direct Mail (or Email) Fundraising Work?

Fundraising shares many evaluation challenges with communication: potential donors receive so much information about your nonprofit that you do not have direct control over. So how do you know which messages are working and whether the strategies that you devote so much time to are driving donations? A/B testing is the most concrete and specific tool at your disposal and is becoming even easier to use amidst the ongoing transition from direct mail to direct email fundraising. So, how can you use A/B testing to understand which of your messages is most effective in driving donations?

A/B Testing: Apples, Oranges, and Important Reminders

A/B testing compares the performance of two or more versions of the same piece of content to determine which is more effective. Remember: the core message remains consistent in each version—you don't want to change so much that you are comparing an apple to an orange. Instead, make minor adjustments to the language or visual presentation to compare a Granny Smith apple to a Gala apple.

For example, one nonprofit sought to influence teacher behavior and was heavily dependent on email messaging. Early on in the program, the theory about email content was that using a teacher's voice would be more effective than an observer's voice. Staff conducted a series of tests using the same story but varying the perspective, using first person versus third person. More specifically, they also tested the signator, using the teacher in one message versus the program staff member in the other. Overwhelmingly, the evidence supported their theory: messages delivered using a teacher's voice had consistently higher open rates, click-through rates and forward rates.

After you have designed two or more versions of a fundraising message, split your distribution list randomly and evenly and send each version to one group. For the A/B Test to be valid, you must split the list randomly—do not cherry pick age groups, zip codes, or specific individuals that you think will be most receptive to a certain message. Direct email platforms make this process easy and have A/B testing built in.

When you are conducting an A/B Test, the most important thing is to link the element that you are varying with the action you are measuring. For example, if you are varying the language or visual presentation *inside* the body of an email, open rate is not the right measure, because readers do not see the body before they decide whether or not to open an email. The two areas that A/B Tests focus on are subject lines for direct email and message content.

Before you begin, use the guidance in this chapter to clarify what you are hoping to learn from an A/B Test. If you decide you want to know, "Which of our core messages drives donations?" focus on message content. If you decide you want to know, "Which of our emails do recipients open most?" focus on subject line and sender. In the table below and the next two sections, we'll talk specifically about which measures to use for each test.

	Direct Mail	Direct Email
Subject Line	Not applicable. You can't know for sure how many people opened a letter.	◆ Open rate
Message Content	◆ Returned donation forms ◆ Website traffic using a custom web address	◆ Click-through rate ◆ Forward rate

Testing Subject Lines

Subject line testing only applies to direct email fundraising. Subject line testing focuses on aspects of a message that drive readers just to open the message. With direct mail, you cannot know how many people opened a piece of mail. Email platforms make this information accessible, and with the open rates reported by every email marketing platform, you are now able to directly test whether variations in the subject line or sender changes how many people open your email. And while this is not a direct indicator of success—the number of people who open an email is not the same as the number of people who donate—your fundraising plea cannot succeed unless people open it.

Testing Message Content

Beyond open rates, variations in message content can drive donor behavior, and you can measure it. In the case of direct mail fundraising, when you include an envelope for recipients to return donations, be sure that the envelopes are marked subtly to distinguish which message they received, so that you can count return rates and amounts for each message. When you include a website for recipients to donate online, include a different URL in each message. While each of the URLs can redirect to the same donation page, the analytics on your website can tell you how many donors originated from each URL.

For direct email fundraising, this process is easier. Every email marketing platform automatically reports two useful indicators: click-through rates when there is an embedded link in an email and forward rates. Which metric you focus on depends on your key evaluation question, discussed in **Chapter Four.** If your priority is donation behavior, then click-through rate is the right indicator, and you should also see a corresponding spike in donations when the email is sent to confirm that recipients are not just clicking the link and leaving without donating. If your priority is whether donors recruit others to donate, forward rate is a great indication. Again, the goal is to compare these rates between two messages with slight variations.

Donor Surveys and Their Effect on Engagement

The second place the development team directly and uniquely uses evaluation is in donor surveys. One nonprofit partner of mine used donor surveys for years as a way to maintain relationships with past donors and encourage repeat donations. But when we sat down and looked at how many donors responded to donor surveys and what proportion of those respondents clicked the donation link in the "thank you for filling out of survey" email, the development director was shocked to learn that her donor engagement survey was having the opposite effect:

Response rates were steadily declining, and the donation link in the thank-you email had the lowest click-through of any direct fundraising messages that year. Even worse, donors were unsubscribing from the email list when they received a survey. Why? Survey fatigue! As we discussed earlier, our modern Survey Monkey times have created an environment when nonprofits survey about absolutely everything, and the people you are trying to survey tune out.

My word of wisdom on this topic is quite simple: surveys are not an effective donor relationship tool. If you are using a survey to maintain relationships, stop. Send donors nice messages, call them and don't survey them. If there are meaningful and substantial things that you would like to learn about your donors, start with **Chapter Four** and read all of **Part Two.** Get clear about what you need to know about your donors and which evaluation methods are the best to answer those questions. Remember, surveys should not be the default: consider what you are trying to learn, and whether other data collection methods might be better to answer those questions. And if a survey is the best approach, it should not also include a donation link: you are already asking them for something, don't push your luck.

Communicating Evaluation with Meaning for the Funder

Now let's transition to the other side of the development and evaluation relationship: how to communicate about evaluation with potential and current funders, including foundations, individuals, and corporations. We begin by exploring some of the hurdles that foundations present in the form of grant evaluation questions:

Foundations: Overcome Impossible Evaluation Questions on Grant Applications

Grant application questions about evaluation can be a nightmare. Here are only a few examples of the many prompts that can rattle your cage:

◆ Describe the organization's overall approach to evaluation.

◆ Describe how the organization measures impact.

◆ Summarize key evaluation results or findings that demonstrate the organization's impact.

◆ What are the measurable outcomes your organization is expecting to achieve? We are looking for the clear and specific anticipated results of your work.

It's hard to figure out what is being asked for overall, let alone what the differences between each question are. Oh, and then there's the word limit to contend with. The good news is that everyone else is confused by these questions, too. So if you provide high-quality, substantive responses—even if they are not quite answering the question that was asked—it can go a long way to setting your application apart.

Here are five tips to help you make friends with the dreaded evaluation section. And if you run into a particularly hairy set of evaluation questions, consider anonymously sending this book to the foundation grant administration: we cover the foundation side of this equation in **Chapter Twelve.**

Avoid the Indicator Rabbit Hole

At its core, evaluation is about learning and generating information to drive program improvement and monitor what difference the program is making. But when asked to identify "measurable indicators of impact," our brains move toward things that are easy to measure, which is not the same as what really matters. The same thing happens when funders ask nonprofits to list expected outputs and outcomes. Does the number of people served really capture the impact of your program? What about the changes in the lives of those that you've served—where is that captured?

When you see a request for specific measurable indicators, or to distinguish between outputs and outcomes, don't take the bait! Start first with figuring out what you really want to learn about your program and how evaluation can help with that. Do you wonder about your program at night? Which components of the program matter most? Which are you least sure about? Start by developing your key evaluation questions, which are the questions you are relying on your evaluation to help you answer. They help keep the focus of an evaluation on what matters.

Chapter Four describes key evaluation questions, and the process to develop them in detail. These key evaluation questions then dictate what makes sense to include as an output. For instance, the tangible things your program produces en route to desired changes, such as people served. An example of an outcome might be the actual changes stipulated in your key evaluation questions, such as people who find employment. And remember, key evaluation questions look different for every organization and every program.

There is no one way to capture impact. For example, new programs often focus more on understanding how their program is working: is it implemented as planned? Is it reaching the intended audience? For new programs, it makes sense to start here and hold more outcome-focused questions until later. If you start with outcomes and find they aren't what you hoped, then you don't know whether the program doesn't work or if it just hasn't been implemented properly.

Recognize That Funders Aren't Evaluation Experts

Most foundations don't know evaluation either. That's why this book has a chapter for them, too. Only the biggest foundations have dedicated evaluation staff. Like you, foundations know it matters, and that they should be using it, but they don't really know how. As a result, application and report questions on evaluation are clunky at best. Application questions have a common goal to understand how strategic and functional an applicant is.

The evaluation questions are no different; by asking how your organization measures impact, foundations don't actually want to hear about your pre- and post-test. They want to understand how you use evaluation strategically to inform and improve your programming. Tell that story. Talk about how evaluation is integrated into your organization, how you thoughtfully constructed key evaluation questions, how you used them to dictate the evaluation tools implemented, and how the findings are integrating into your program planning.

Align Evaluation Expectations and Resources

I see a chronic mismatch between the evaluation nonprofits want and the resources they have available. Evaluation is not free, whether done by an external evaluator or internally by the organization. Internally run evaluations cost the organization more in staffing time, whereas external evaluations require contracting dollars. And the two are not mutually exclusive: external evaluations still require staff time, most often for planning and data collection, and it can be wise to engage external support to build capacity for internal evaluation.

Consider the capacity of your team, both their evaluation expertise and their bandwidth, before deciding which route to go. The rule of thumb is that evaluation should be 10 percent of the program budget—not the grant budget—or $5,000, whichever is larger. I regularly hear, "But Elena, we don't have that kind of money for evaluation," to which I say, "If it is important enough to do, it is important enough to evaluate, and part of your role is advocating for the resources your nonprofit needs." Funders are asking you for evaluation, so it's time to ask them to put money behind it.

Treat Evaluation as a Team Effort

Evaluation is a team sport. It cannot be planned, executed, or reported well alone. Be sure to involve program staff, grant managers, your executive director, and perhaps even your board in shaping your evaluation plans, and share this book with them. The most important people to collaborate with are those responsible for implementing the program, as well as those charged with making sure the evaluation happens. You need to understand what capacity they have for evaluation, and they need to understand what is being promised in the grant. I also strongly recommend that you consult with an evaluator before submitting any plans. Evaluators can provide an important "reality check" on whether your plans and your resources are aligned.

Let Your Program Drive the Evaluation

How many times have you had a program change after the grant application was submitted? The same thing happens with evaluation. As programs change, so should the evaluation. When crafting evaluation language for a proposal, stay high-level. Focus on your key evaluation questions and a general sense of what types of data will help answer those questions. Avoid promising specific methods and results, especially the kitchen-sink approach of listing everything that you could do.

You've Won the Grant: How Do You Report Your Findings?

You've won the grant, congratulations! You make sure the funds are successfully delivered and then pass the baton on to your program colleagues. For some organizations, that might be the last development staff will hear until reporting time. For others, the development staff take a leading role in making sure that the grant deliverables are met. Either way, after a year, it's time for the grant report...and here come the evaluation questions again.

At this point, there is pressure not only to convince funders that you are worthy of funding, but that their support makes a difference: the framing of grant reports presuppose positive evaluation results! It feels like a losing battle: no evaluation has entirely good findings, but presenting less-than-ideal evaluation results feels the same as saying that your organization is not effective. So, how can you, instead, infuse a learning orientation into the way you present your evaluation findings? In other words, how can you make it clear that the strength of your organization is that you learn and evolve every year? That you take those less than ideal results and improve your services. Let's review three strategies to help you convey your findings in this way:

Use Data Sandwiches to Structure the Data

In **Chapter Seven,** I introduced the concept of a data sandwich to structure your evaluation results in a way that highlights the "So What?" for readers. That approach is low-hanging fruit to improve your grant reports. I recommend rereading that section before continuing.

Find the Value in Negative Results

Never in my career have I seen an evaluation that was either all good or all bad. Every evaluation has results to be proud of and results for you to learn from, and that is exactly the point: negative results are not a bad thing. I know it doesn't feel like that when you first see the data. You've worked hard and believe in the work you are doing. Finding out that things are not going as well as you had hoped can be soul crushing. After you have seen the data, take one day before writing anything about it for a report.

Then, with your program and leadership colleagues, capitalize on the opportunity that negative results present: to learn, grow, and improve your programs. Because at the end of the day, funders do not want or expect perfect evaluation results. Funders want to hear what didn't work and how you will learn from it in the future. One of my favorite foundation partners says over and over again, "If our grantees aren't learning, we can't learn." And, a 2017 study from the Center for Effective Philanthropy found that 95 percent of foundation program officers see learning from grantees as an integral part of their jobs.

Resist the Temptation to Rinse and Repeat

Once you finish writing up your evaluation results for the grant, resist the urge to copy and paste the same evaluation plan into next year's grant application. Evaluation plans should shift and evolve over time. Revisit your key evaluation questions: have they been answered? Or, do they remain open questions? Did your findings generate new questions? Use this year's evaluation results to drive next year's key evaluation questions: what has been answered thoroughly can be removed, what remains unanswered stays, and what emerged gets added.

Individual Donors: Get Ahead of the Evaluation Conversation

While professionally staffed foundations have been evaluation-aware since at least the early 2000s, individual donors and family foundations have not yet started asking about evaluation en masse. So you might be tempted to say, "Great, I don't have to talk to them about evaluation." But here's the thing: because individuals haven't started asking yet, nonprofits have an opportunity to frame the evaluation conversation productively from the start, unlike what's happened with foundations. It is only a matter of time before evaluation starts popping up in conversations with individual donors: why not take control of the conversation? Instead of avoiding the conversation until you are forced to have it, how do you preempt the conversation and set yourself apart from other nonprofits with your evaluation know-how?

Let me tell you a story about a local Colorado nonprofit that uses this strategy to tremendous effect. Normally, fundraising galas and luncheons follow a very similar pattern: emotional plea by the staff, testimonial by a client, famous keynote speaker, an auction, and some donation asks at each table. Rarely does evaluation get a cameo appearance, let alone a starring role. So when I went to a fundraising luncheon in 2016, I expected the usual song and dance. Instead, the board chair and executive director introduced evaluation at the very beginning, and throughout the lunch evaluation, continued making appearances. And the fundraising ask on each table? It included a full page on the nonprofit's evaluation approach. The organization framed its commitment to evaluation as evidence of strategic and impactful programming.

The message was: we care about the kids we serve so much that we prioritize ongoing evaluation to learn what's working and what's not. We use that information to tweak and refine our programs and to share that information with others trying to do similar work. Because the kids are more important than any allegiance we have to a particular program model, and we want to do what's best for them. My jaw dropped. And I wasn't alone. After the event I did some digging and discovered that this organization had built a reputation for a strong commitment to program evaluation—and that its evaluation commitment was a driving factor for repeat donors and major gifts.

So how do you emulate this approach with your individual donors? I'll share three areas of "low-hanging fruit" to spark your creativity about how to incorporate evaluation into your fundraising messaging.

Support an Emotional Plea with Evaluation

Emotional staff pleas and client testimonials are unlikely to disappear from individual donor asks. But they aren't enough. As donors increase in sophistication and younger impact-focused donors increase their charitable contributions, we are seeing a higher degree of skepticism about these emotional messages year after year. Once you've established the need for your services through emotions, use evaluation evidence to justify that you are the right organization to address the issue and demonstrate that you are making progress. The ideal message for individual donors includes both: emotions get you in the door, and evidence seals the deal.

Emphasize Evaluation as a Part of Programming

Sometimes I get pushback from development staff who don't want to talk about evaluation because individual donors don't like the idea that some of their money goes to non-programming expenses. My contention is that evaluation is a programming expense. Evaluation helps make sure the program is improving and achieving what the donors are supporting you to do. And that's the message to use with individual donors: evaluation is a critical piece of our program, just like staffing and facilities. Without evaluation, we won't be able to deliver on the expectations you have for us.

Be Prepared to Provide Some Light Evaluation Education

Some individual donors have taken the return on investment question a little bit too far. And unfortunately being on the leading edge of how nonprofits use and communicate about evaluation requires some ongoing education for those who aren't quite there yet. The overarching response to any pushback you get from individual donors about the specific return on their investment is that social impact doesn't work like that. Complex issues require complex evaluation and messy work generates messy answers.

Take this opportunity to help your donors understand a little more about how you think about evaluation. Share your favorite passage from **Parts One** and **Two** of this book and draw on the lessons from return on investment conversations at the board level in **Chapter Eleven.** Be sure to emphasize the ways in which you do use evaluation strategically and the information that you can share about the impact of their investment when combined with other investments.

Corporations: Promote Alignment and Impact

The last group you might have evaluation conversations with are corporations, particularly those with structured Corporate Social Responsibility (CSR) programs. In some ways, these conversations overlap with the advice I just shared on individual donors: like individuals, corporations have not yet fully arrived at the evaluation party, so you have more ability to guide the conversation than with funders. And like individuals, corporations come at the evaluation conversation from outside the nonprofit field, which can sometimes lead to some sticking points and confusion. The first step is to understand the corporation's motivation for supporting nonprofit programs. The answer to that question determines the best way to approach the conversation: focus on brand alignment or focus on true impact. Let's explore three relevant ideas.

Determining Corporate Funder Motivation

Corporations invest in nonprofits for different reasons. Some believe they have an opportunity to leverage resources to make a difference in their communities. Others see CSR as a branding opportunity to show how socially aware and community-involved they are while providing a great volunteer opportunity for their staff. These two motivations dictate very different approaches to talking to corporations about evaluation.

Generally, all corporations will start by saying that they want to make an impact. Dig deeper: ask your potential corporate funders what a successful nonprofit partnership looks like. Do they talk about marketing materials, staff donations, volunteer days, etc.? Or do they talk about changing the community around them? If the former, focus on how evaluation can help align their CSR programs with their brands. If the latter, focus on how your organization has implemented best practices in nonprofit program evaluation and how that looks different than how they evaluate for-profit initiatives.

Selling Brand Alignment

For corporations that are most interested in supporting nonprofits to show how socially aware and community involved they are, the evaluation conversation can remain minimal. Use some of the language in the preceding section for individual donors about how evaluation helps you do your work better. Then, if corporations take pride in being strategic and "data-driven," use evaluation to demonstrate that you are results-oriented, too. Data-driven companies supporting data-driven nonprofits to improve the communities in which they both work—what could be a better marketing message?

Promoting True Impact in the Community

If, however, corporations are deeply and authentically invested in making a true difference in their communities, let evaluation take up more space in the conversation. Like individual donors mentioned above and board members in **Chapter Eleven,** corporations need some help understanding how impact in the nonprofit world is different than impact in the business world. Many corporate funders want clear and tangible return on their investment, much like the way businesses look for an increase in profit or profit margin on new business lines.

As you've learned throughout this book, that doesn't exist for most social programs. In my experience, the most successful evaluation conversations steer the conversation away from how businesses think about impact to the best practices in nonprofit evaluation. The risk of engaging in the return-on-investment conversation is that you end up promising a level of concrete evidence that you are unable to deliver. Instead, help the corporation understand what impact measurement looks like for complex social programs and how well-aligned your evaluation is with the field's best practices.

At this point, I hope you've found a few useful tips to strengthen how your development team uses evaluation. What one thing can you take away and immediately implement in your organization? Hand this book and your evaluation commitment off to the board of directors of your organization.

Chapter Eleven

The Board of Directors

L et's say you joined a nonprofit board because you want to give back to the community. You care deeply about the nonprofit's mission, and at some point during your board service, you start to wonder, "Well, are we doing any good?" That's where evaluation comes in: evaluation is the tool that nonprofits use to assess whether what they are doing is helping improve their communities.

This chapter gives you the information you need to engage productively in conversations about evaluation at the nonprofit whose board you serve on. At the board level, "How are we doing?" can be interpreted as, "How is the nonprofit doing or how is the board doing?" so we cover both in this chapter. First, we briefly discuss how boards evaluate themselves and their contributions. Then we dive more deeply into how boards can support and encourage evaluation of the whole nonprofit and its work.

Education to Action

Let's look at the board of Education to Action, a public media nonprofit that uses education and awareness to drive civic action. To give you a little context, most public media say they are successful if their Nielsen ratings are high and they have enough money in the budget to do their work. Yet, neither ratings nor donations speak to whether or not these nonprofits are doing anything good for viewers with their funding. Sure, there were substantial evaluations of specific programming vehicles, most notably, the educational and development outcomes of Sesame Street. But for public media nonprofits as a whole, evaluations started and ended with providing access to educational content. When Education to

Action hired a new CEO, Claire, she had big ideas and aspirations for how a public media nonprofit could go beyond just producing content and start using that content to drive civic action.

To Claire, evaluation was key to this strategy: without evaluation, how could Education to Action know what types of content drove civic action and which didn't, so as to skew the mix towards action over time? Education to Action's board was bought into Claire's overall strategy of using public media to drive civic action. After all, they hired her. But they weren't sold on how evaluation could help. Education to Action had a larger than typical board with twenty-one members. The members were split between business experts predominantly from the media and technology space and nonprofit or public sector experts. The business experts liked the Nielsen-ratings approach to evaluation because it looked familiar: viewership, website visits, and financial indicators. That's what they tracked in their companies, so it seemed sufficient for Education to Action.

The nonprofit and public sector experts knew that those traditional indicators wouldn't cut it in the new universe of using public media to drive civic action. They understood that even if the nonprofit was financially strong and people were watching the shows or visiting the website, those facts said nothing about whether Education to Action was moving viewers to act. And they didn't think anything could help them measure that question. In the past, the nonprofit and public sector experts tried to use evaluation for aspirational social change like civic action, yet they always felt let down by the lack of insights into the results. In the end, they determined it was best to hire experts on developing content that drives action and trust them to make an impact.

Claire was not satisfied with these perspectives. It was true that she had never seen an evaluation of public media's ability to drive civic action. But she still thought it could be done. And she needed more data to justify content decisions that weren't just an expert's opinion. Claire was referred to me, and we started to work together to craft an evaluation strategy for Education to Action above and beyond traditional public media evaluation. We decided early on that bringing the board along in this process was going to be critical to the success of the evaluation. So after I guided the internal leadership team through the process in **Part Two,** Claire and I planned educational sessions and dialogues for the board.

The initial conversation stirred up the bias and resistance we expected based on the board's professional backgrounds and experiences. But after providing new ways of thinking and talking about evaluation, we started to feel a shift in the room. I walked the board through the framing language around evaluation in **Chapter Two** and described the process we went through as a leadership team to get to the evaluation framework we were proposing that day. Claire shared the key evaluation question that mattered most: to what extent does Education to Action content drive audience members to take civic action? What types of content are most effective?

The board vigorously agreed that these questions addressed the core unknowns. Then I shared the evaluation plan for the upcoming years that would help us answer those key questions. While still skeptical, the majority of the board felt a glimmer of hope that we might actually be able to build an evaluation strategy to understand whether and how Education to Action was driving civic action. *And how cool if we could.*

From then on, the board was generally supportive of Claire's evaluation priorities and plans. They approved the original budget she asked for and assisted in fundraising for future additions. They asked supportive, learning-oriented questions about the evaluation process. And they stopped using Nielsen ratings and financial indicators as evidence that the nonprofit was "effective." Instead, the full board and leadership team recognized that while they didn't currently know whether the nonprofit was effective, they were going to find out. Together.

Evaluating Yourselves

Just as programs have different goals that require different structures and activities, boards take different forms for different goals. Evaluating a board that primarily serves a fundraising purpose looks different than evaluating a working board or a policy-setting board. Similarly, a higher level of engagement and activity is reasonable to ask of a board that meets monthly than of one that meets quarterly. You see where I am going here? Just like the process for program evaluation started with mapping the program in **Chapter Three,** evaluating a nonprofit board has to first start with understanding the board's meeting frequency and primary purpose.

You cannot just use the first board assessment that Google spits out and expect it to garner useful information. First, consider the board's primary function: What is the board expected to do? Why is that the right area of contribution for the board? Does it fill gaps in staff expertise? How often does the board meet? What are members expected to do between board meetings? After you are clear about the function and structure of your board of directors, seek a board assessment that matches.

Speak with other nonprofits that have similarly structured boards and see if they have had positive experience with a board assessment tool in the past. Reach out to an expert in board governance for assessment recommendations. Generally, you want to find a membership assessment that looks at things like demographics and skills that individual board members bring to the table, and a competency-based assessment that looks at the performance and contributions of the board.

The work does not stop when you've completed the assessment! Don't simply take the assessment—pat yourselves on the back for the areas you excel, ignore the areas you don't, and move on with your lives. The value of evaluating yourselves is in the conversations about the results. It's the conversations that can lead to better performance in the future. Follow the guidance in **Chapter Seven** to actively engage with the results and reflect on where tweaks and improvements are needed. Then share the takeaways from this reflection with the nonprofit staff you support: nothing is a stronger endorsement of meaningful evaluation than practicing what you preach.

Asking Productive Questions about Nonprofit Evaluation

As we discussed in **Part One**, everyone in the nonprofit sector has a different understanding of what evaluation is and different emotional baggage from past evaluation experiences. For some, evaluation is loved and seen as the secret to nonprofit success. For others, it's a burden of data collection that doesn't help anything and just gets in the way of direct service delivery. This diversity of perspectives on evaluation is heightened among board members.

Why? Because not all board members have day jobs in the nonprofit sector. Boards bring together professionals from an array of industries, and many of those industries have their own version of evaluation. Financial professionals are most familiar with dashboards and measuring actual figures against budget projections. Business professionals are most familiar with key performance indicators and setting SMART goals for product development. Lawyers are most familiar with thresholds of truth in terms of logical and convincing arguments, and using data from physical evidence, expert testimony, and witness testimony.

Each of these professionals brings a unique background to a conversation about evaluation in the nonprofit boardroom and, suddenly, you have a room full of people saying similar words to express different concepts. In the upcoming sections, we explore tips for overcoming this difference in language and background to transform your board of directors into a productive partner in the evaluation process.

Setting the Playing Field: What Is Nonprofit Evaluation?

The first step when it comes to boards and evaluation is to understand what evaluation is, how it is used in the context of nonprofit work, and the value of implementing meaningful evaluation strategies. This step alone can take multiple tries because, after every board meeting, members go back to their day jobs and continue to get experience and education in their field's version of evaluation. With a single conversation about evaluation, it is nearly impossible to drown out that messaging. Also, board meetings rarely have full attendance. Even one board member who misses the nonprofit evaluation memo can derail productive conversations about evaluation. I recommend you share this chapter with as many fellow board members as possible. Now let's discuss how nonprofit evaluation differs from other forms of evaluation and the support systems that should be in place.

Nonprofit Evaluation Is Focused on Learning

So, what's the best way for board members to conceptualize evaluation? Evaluation in a nonprofit context is more often than not unlike evaluation in board members' professional and personal lives. In their professional lives, most board members think of evaluation in terms of monitoring impact, financial evaluation or return on investment, and personnel evaluation or performance management. Which one comes to mind first when you think of evaluation? All three of these examples assume a lens of accountability: making sure that someone or some nonprofit is doing what it says it is.

But nonprofit work is messier than that—it's rarely clear what "should be doing" is. Changing social outcomes and contexts is complex and very few nonprofits have a simple causal link between what they do and the changes they see in the world. For example, literacy programs that seek to increase students' reading proficiency on the surface seem simple: you tutor kids at a critical age and their reading scores increase. But in reality, that logic underestimates all the other things happening in kids' lives, like their teacher, their interest in the material, their lives outside the classroom, and even something like how severe the flu season is that year.

How we wish the world would work

TUTORING **READING PROFICIENCY**

How the world actually works

FLU SEASON

FAMILY CONTEXT

TUTORING **READING PROFICIENCY**

QUALITY OF TEACHING

STUDENT INTEREST IN MATERIALS

Because nonprofit work is so messy, an accountability approach is detached from reality and a waste of time for both the board and the nonprofit staff. And, unfortunately, an accountability approach is not net-neutral: it can actually do serious damage to the relationship between a nonprofit board and the nonprofit staff, which is counterproductive to enhancing the nonprofit's effectiveness. Think about the assumptions behind taking an accountability lens to evaluation: evaluation as accountability implies that there is a right way of approaching this work, that the board knows what that is, and that the staff are simply not doing it right.

Now put yourself in the shoes of the nonprofit staff. Is that a relationship that would help you do your job better? Instead, I encourage board members to think of themselves as partners in the learning journey that is evaluation. Instead of approaching evaluation by setting strict guidelines about what should be done and asking the staff to report on whether or not those things are happening, work through **Part Two** of this book with the nonprofit staff and jointly select the priority learning questions to guide the evaluation work.

Nonprofit Evaluation Is Systematic

Now, remember I said nonprofit evaluation is different than evaluation in board members' professional *and* personal lives. On the personal side, we are all evaluators in our everyday lives. According to the dictionary, evaluation is "the making of a judgment about the amount, number or value or something." In our everyday life, there is no need for the judgment to have methodological rigor and defensibility because each individual can make those judgments individually.

If you read a rave movie review, you can go see the movie and decide whether you agree. If you like the movie, too, you might trust the reviewer's judgment in the future. And if you don't, you might read a different reviewer in the future. But with nonprofit programs, we cannot experience programs for ourselves. You will never be able to experience a fourth-grade reading program for yourself. So, the evaluation of that fourth-grade reading program must show its accuracy and reliability in other ways. Nonprofit evaluation has to use rigorous, defensible, and contextually appropriate approaches to ensure the veracity of end judgments.

A learning-oriented evaluation that's rigorous and defensible is the secret to making good nonprofit evaluation magical. At the end of the day, nonprofit evaluation is a process of systematically understanding whether your nonprofit's programming works. And if so, why does it work? For whom? Under what conditions? And how can we make it better? The answers to these questions not only can help you monitor mission achievement, but they can also motivate funders and donors, improve services, and increase your impact in the community.

Now that you see what nonprofit evaluation is, why it matters, and how it differs from what you think of evaluation in your professional and personal experiences, how do you support your nonprofit in developing an evaluation framework and get clarity?

Supporting the Development of an Evaluation Framework

The core message of this book is *to focus on the learning questions that evaluation can answer, the what and why that precedes the methods and metrics of evaluation, and the how of evaluation.* This is the most important piece of advice that I will continue to shout from the rooftops: "What are you learning about your programs?" and "Why is your evaluation focused on those areas?" are far more helpful questions than "How are you measuring that?" and "How do we know it's working?"

Getting Clear on the Focus of the Evaluation

Once you redirect the conversation from metrics to learnings, the first question to answer is whose learning questions are the priority. Nonprofits have a tendency to focus first on what their funders need, second on what their boards ask, and third, if at all, on what their front-line staff need to know to do their jobs better. One of the most helpful things a board can do to support a nonprofit's evaluation is to encourage the nonprofit to flip that order on its head.

Ask the staff first about what they want to know. What do they not know about their programs? What missing nuggets of information would help them do their jobs better? What keeps them up at night? You'll notice that these are very intimidating questions to be asked by your board of directors unless you have first done the legwork to acculturate evaluation as a learning tool rather than an accountability measure. When the board is a partner in the nonprofit's learning, these questions become fodder for great conversation. When the board is an accountability check, these questions quickly escalate into defensiveness, fear, and conflict.

Share the resources in this book with the nonprofit staff and encourage them to go through the process outlined in **Part Two.** After you have a clear understanding of what the nonprofit staff want to learn from evaluation, think about what, if anything, the board needs to learn. Ninety-nine times out of a hundred, I have found that after the nonprofit staff go through the careful process outlined in **Chapter Four,** the areas of highest priority to the board are already on the list. If not, flip back to **Chapter Four** and go through the exercise as a board. Have a conversation with the nonprofit staff about whether they considered the questions you came up with. And come to a consensus about how to prioritize resources—don't just combine their list of questions with yours because:

Evaluation Costs Money

Whether the nonprofit decides to do the evaluation in-house or hire an external consultant to support it, evaluation is expensive. Before you jump head first into evaluation, take a moment to assess whether your nonprofit has the capacity to do it well. I like to focus on three considerations:

Are We Ready to Tweak the Program Based on Evaluation Results?

If evaluation is not going to change what you do, then why spend the resources to do it?

Do We Have Staff with Evaluation Expertise?

A myth about evaluation is that anyone with a data mindset can do it. I am a huge proponent of the idea that anyone can learn how to be an evaluator, however, when nonprofits are implementing meaningful evaluation for the first time, they need someone who is already an evaluator. If you don't have an evaluator on staff, draw on external support. You can hire an evaluator to do the whole thing for you, provide some capacity building in evaluation to help you do the evaluation internally, or a combination of the two. The American Evaluation Association has an extensive list of evaluators for reference.

Do We Have Financial Resources to Dedicate to Evaluation?

Whether your nonprofit conducts the evaluation internally or hires an external evaluator, evaluation requires dedicated resources. Do you know how much your nonprofit spends on evaluation? Remember, the rule of thumb is that evaluation should be 10 percent of the program budget— not the grant budget—or $5,000, whichever is larger. Consider asking the nonprofit to give evaluation its own budget line item on financial reports, so the board can easily monitor changes in evaluation expenditures over time. While monitoring the budget line item for evaluation may feel like a finite task, let's balance the scales by turning our attention to a job that requires keeping an open mind.

Keep an Open Mind About Data

Once you have narrowed the learning focus for the evaluation and set a reasonable budget to support it, it is up the nonprofit staff to develop the evaluation method. But remember that the approach they come back to you with might look different than you expect. Nonprofit evaluation is more than just surveys and counting data! Evaluators commonly use paper and electronic surveys, interviews, focus groups, observation, and secondary documents and data.

Which type of data is most appropriate depends on the key evaluation questions you have selected. Many of us are naturally driven toward hard numbers, but remember, not everything should be quantified. Quantitative data is great when you want to generalize, replicate, and test an experience that you already understand well. When it comes to new terrain, emotionally sensitive topics, and capturing the "how" and "why" of program outcomes, qualitative data shines. One of the most important things a board can do to support nonprofit evaluation is to keep an open mind about data sources that are unfamiliar.

Engaging with Evaluation Results

We've talked about getting started with evaluation, but now let's talk about what happens when the evaluation results come back in. I'd encourage you to schedule a refresher on evaluation as a learning process during the meeting before evaluation results come in, using a recap or recording of

A Word of Caution About Dashboards

Every nonprofit board wants a dashboard to succinctly summarize key nonprofit metrics, and often they want impact included on this dashboard. If the chapter up to this point has not yet dissuaded you from asking for an impact dashboard, let me be direct. Dashboards are rarely the right approach to nonprofit evaluation, and more often than not they are counterproductive to having a useful conversation about nonprofit impact.

Why? First, because dashboards prioritize clear and tangible quantitative metrics. Great for finances, terrible for complicated social change efforts. Second, nonprofit impact does not change on the same timeline as board meetings. If board members meet every month, they are likely to see a dashboard that is a mirror image of what they saw the month before. Because social change takes time. Third, dashboards are an accountability tool, they set what "should be done" and measure current work against that bar. When a board forces the use of a dashboard, the nonprofit responds by creating a dashboard with the things that can easily be measured, like the number of people served. And at first, the board is happy, "Yay, we have an impact dashboard." But soon they start to look closer and realize that what's reported on the dashboard reflects what can be measured, not what matters. It's easy to then blame the nonprofit for not having meaningful metrics, but really, the blame falls on the request: dashboards are not the right format for meaningful evaluation.

your past evaluation conversations. Since boards are not usually involved in the execution of an evaluation, there can be a long gap between evaluation-planning conversations and evaluation-results conversations. It can be easy to fall back into the old habit of evaluation as accountability during that gap. Let's correct that habit and take a closer look at learning and strategy:

Questions About Learning

After the nonprofit staff share the evaluation results with you, take the opportunity to start a conversation. Some board meetings are structured more as a passive download of information: the staff present, the board approves, next topic. Evaluation can't function like that. For the board to be a productive partner in the evaluation process, you need to dedicate the time and space for a real discussion.

Often the nonprofits I work with schedule the evaluation presentation during the month before the board retreat. They use the regular board meeting to present the evaluation findings and the retreat to have a deeper conversation about the implications of those findings. If you use an external evaluation partner, this structure is ideal, because the evaluation contractor can come to the regular meeting to share the details of the evaluation but leave the deeper strategic conversation to the staff and board alone at the retreat.

As a board member, your role in this part of the evaluation process is to ask good questions that push the nonprofit staff's thinking forward, and then to support the strategic decisions that come from those conversations. Here's a cheat sheet of universally applicable questions about evaluation. Start here, then continue the conversation with questions specific to the nonprofit's work. For more details on the full learning and reflection cycle, not just conversations at the board level, check out **Chapter Seven.**

◆ What are the answers to our key evaluation questions, if you had to summarize each in one sentence?

◆ What does the data tell us about our work?

◆ Does this align with your expectations?

◆ Where are the surprises?

◆ What about our program do we want to make sure not to lose?

◆ What changes to our programming might make sense?

◆ Who should we share these results with? How? When?

◆ What new questions does this evaluation raise?

Always remember our early conversation about how damaging an accountability-focused evaluation conversation can be on the board-staff relationship. If you are the board chair, it is your responsibility to guide board member questions away from accountability if they start to stray in that direction. I'd recommend reminding the board of that framing at the beginning of the conversation and gently remind individual members of that learning orientation if an accountability question comes up.

Evolving the Evaluation Strategy

A common myth about nonprofit evaluation is that nonprofits should do the same evaluation every year. "We need longitudinal comparative data, right?" Not so. You only need to repeat an evaluation year after year if a longitudinal comparison is necessary for the key evaluation questions you are trying to answer. For all other questions, this approach is accountability slipping in again. Evaluation as learning should evolve and change as you learn more about the nonprofit's work.

As the last question on the list above suggests, a good evaluation generates more questions than it answers. The conversation you have with staff about their evaluation results should encourage shifting the evaluation strategy in response to new information. Which key evaluation questions feel sufficiently answered? Take those off the list. Which key evaluation questions still feel ambiguous? Do they still feel important to get clearer answers to? What new questions emerged from this evaluation?

After you have a revised set of key evaluation questions, revisit the evaluation budget. As your questions evolve, so might the resource intensity of answering them. We often find that as nonprofits start to learn from evaluation results, they want deeper, richer information, and that costs more to do well. It is not uncommon for an evaluation budget to increase over time, but I have also seen the reverse, where the first year's evaluation answers so many questions that the nonprofit takes a lighter touch approach with a smaller budget the next year.

Sharing Results

Your last critical role as a board partner in the evaluation process is to encourage nonprofits to share their results. I share detailed best practices for how and with whom evaluation findings should be shared in **Chapter Seven.** The board should first play a role in making it okay to share the good and the bad from the evaluation results.

Often nonprofits are afraid to share any information that makes them seem less than perfect, but with the right framing, sharing what you are learning and how you are adapting your programming in response to discoveries can be a powerful demonstration of a nonprofit living its values. And it can have a positive trickle-down effect in the field: as nonprofits share evaluation results, their partners working in the same content area learn, too, and the field gets smarter together. Encourage your nonprofit to set the trend of sharing your full evaluation findings.

Second, the board should play a role in making sure that the nonprofit actually shares with the stakeholders what they say they will. Here is where accountability is actually quite useful: because it is such a deviation from the norm to share evaluation results publicly, it is common for nonprofits to agree to share while in the boardroom, then to chicken out when they get back to the office. As a board member, there is power in regular questioning and following up. Use the second to last question in the bulleted list above to ask nonprofits to set a timeline for sharing the evaluation results, and if those dates come and go without the results being shared, ask them about it.

At this point, I hope you've found a few useful tips to strengthen how your board of directors engages in evaluation. What one thing can you take away and immediately implement in your nonprofit? Hand this book and your evaluation commitment off to the foundations that support your nonprofit.

Chapter Twelve

Foundations

The last evaluation-related role we will focus on is that of the foundations who support nonprofit programming. We begin by talking about how foundations evaluate themselves. Then we cover how foundations evaluate their grantees. The goal of both levels of evaluation is the same: how can foundations and nonprofits come together to understand what's working and what's not, and to use that information to strengthen programs that in turn strengthen our communities?

As a foundation, you hold the purse strings for nonprofit partners. And while you're on the other side of the table, you still care deeply about the communities you serve and want to be the best funding partner you can. You keep an eye on emerging best practices and trends in the foundation community. You communicate regularly with the nonprofits you fund to keep a pulse on their needs and any shifts in the nonprofit landscape. You work hard to fund the right things and to be a thought partner for those funded programs. And yet, you're still not sure if what you are doing is having a positive impact. You can do all the "right" things when making funding decisions, but without thoughtful consideration of evaluation and how it applies in a funding context that uncertainty persists.

Healthy Huerfano

Consider Healthy Huerfano, a brand-new health foundation with a small rural service region. Healthy Huerfano's inaugural board did extensive legwork to understand the most pressing health needs in the community and used those needs to inform the selection of funding priorities. They conducted a series of focus groups with community members, researched promising practices, and spoke with the leadership of other health foundations throughout the country. Once they identified four priority funding areas, they hired Maria, a native of the region with a master's degree in public health and a deep dedication to making Healthy Huerfano an exemplar of an effective foundation and a trusted community partner.

Maria established Healthy Huerfano's funding processes to align with best practices in philanthropy with the addition of unique personal touches, reflecting the culture of the community. Quickly the nonprofit built up a positive reputation in the region and awarded $5 million in grants in its first year. But Maria was not yet satisfied. In her mind, there was a missing piece: evaluation. How would Healthy Huerfano know its funding was improving the health of the region?

The Healthy Huerfano board had some wacky ideas about evaluation. Most notably, they insisted that if the nonprofit were successful, the obesity rates in the region would decrease, so that was the only measure of success that the nonprofit needed. Maria pushed back, trying to explain the plethora of challenges with that approach. The timeline is too far out. There are too many other factors that influence obesity rate. We are a small fish in a pool of big health foundations. And so on, until she realized that she was not making much progress and she had reached the limits of her expertise in evaluation. To push back on her board's unrealistic expectations, she needed some backup.

At that point, Maria reached out to the evaluation director at the largest foundation in the state, who put her in touch with me. Over the course of six months, Maria and I worked closely together to develop an evaluation strategy that would help Healthy Huerfano understand if and how it was making an impact in the community, but that was appropriate for the nascency and size of the nonprofit. As part of this process, we walked through the approach in **Part Two** of this book and got clarity on what the nonprofit needed to know and how to get that information. And we built in a whole lot of board education, drawing on the materials in **Chapter Eleven.** After two sessions with the board and clarity on the needed evaluation structure, the board and Maria jointly decided that the evaluation was beyond their internal capacities and hired my team to execute it. Spoiler alert: the evaluation did not include attributing the obesity rate to the foundation.

In the first year, Healthy Huerfano was able to pilot a new evaluation process and use the findings to inform future changes in the way it worked. In the second year, the focus of evaluation shifted as it should, following the process outlined in **Chapter Seven.** Now, the board, the staff, the local community, and the foundation community recognize the sophistication of Healthy Huerfano's evaluation approach. Not because it is the most rigorous evaluation out there, but because it navigates the challenges of evaluating foundation work with grace to produce information useful to itself and to the larger community.

Evaluating the Foundation

To date, foundations have predominantly focused on evaluating their grantees and not themselves. This disparity furthers the power dynamic already rampant in the foundation and grantee relationship by positioning nonprofit work as something that may or may not be working and the foundation work as above evaluation. Luckily, this is starting to change. Foundations are starting to focus the lens on themselves and practice what they preach by implementing a learning-oriented evaluation approach to their own practices. Specifically, they are starting to look more at how their decisions and systems impact the grantees they serve, treating the grantees as the beneficiaries of foundation programs and processes. You have an opportunity to be on the front lines of this change, so where do you start?

Using Perception Reports to Gauge Foundation Processes

If you are new to evaluating your foundation, one of the easiest ways to get started is by using the Center for Effective Philanthropy (CEP) Perception Reports. CEP has four proprietary assessment tools to measure grantee, applicant, donor, and staff perceptions of a foundation. And what makes CEP's work so valuable is the benchmarking available. Take, for example, the Grantee Perception Report. At the time this book was written, over 250 foundations had used the Grantee Perception Report through CEP. This bank of data allows CEP to provide customized comparisons for your foundation. If you are a private health foundation with less than a $100 million endowment, CEP can provide a comparison of your data to all foundations and to all private health foundations with less than a $100 million endowment.

I have yet to find a perception report that comes close to the power of CEP's benchmarking and the team's understanding of foundation perceptions. Once you have done perception reports for hundreds of foundations, you gain an unparalleled depth of understanding of what a strong foundation-grantee relationship looks like, what is reasonable to expect for different types and maturities of foundations, and when changes can have the most impact. But, CEP's perception reports are expensive. Sometimes prohibitively expensive for smaller foundations. So what else is out there?

Using Program Evaluation Strategies to Evaluate Foundations

If CEP's perception reports are out of your reach right now, fear not—you can build an evaluation of the foundation and its relationships with key stakeholders without using CEP's proprietary tools and benchmarks. How? By using the same process outlined in **Part Two** for program evaluation!

Mapping your program	Does your definition of the foundation's work include: ◆ Funding? ◆ Communications? ◆ Advocacy? ◆ Relationships?
Defining your questions	What do you want to learn? Consider: ◆ Perceptions of the foundation or foundation processes ◆ Sustainability of grantee nonprofits ◆ Building capacity in grantee nonprofits
Matching methods to questions	What methods are best for your questions? Think beyond surveys to consider: ◆ Interviews ◆ Focus groups ◆ Website usability testing

First, make sure that everyone is on the same page about what you mean by "the foundation's work." Are you including your communications work, policy advocacy, and community relationships? Or just your grant funding?

Second, articulate what you are hoping to learn from an evaluation of the foundation. The evaluation planning process for a foundation is the same as for any nonprofit program, as are the evaluation methods used, but the difference is in the questions that you focus on. One foundation I work with articulated its key evaluation question as: "How do past and current grantees perceive the foundation?" This was its first inquiry into grantee perceptions, so the open-ended exploratory approach fit. Another focused on: "How do grantees define sustainability for their nonprofits? And how does the foundation help or hinder sustainability efforts?" This foundation was experienced with evaluating its own work broadly and hoped to now gain a specific understanding of its impact on key nonprofit success factors. And a third selected: "In what ways is the foundation building capacity among local nonprofits? In what ways are we not?" This foundation had articulated in step one that its capacity building work was more important to the community than grant funding, and its key evaluation questions match that realization.

Third, use the key evaluation questions you select to dictate the methods you use in the evaluation. Each of the three foundations above needed very different evaluation methods. For the first, my team and I used a series of focus groups with current and past grantees at a specific point in time. For the second, we did exit interviews with grantees as their grant ended or renewed. And for the third, we used an annual survey to capture baseline capacity and changes in capacity each year, combined with varying evaluation tools for each capacity building event. I've also used website usability testing for evaluation questions specific to perceptions and usability of the grant application process.

Once you are ready to execute the evaluation, foundations must be wary of the power dynamic between foundation staff and nonprofits. Imagine you are a nonprofit executive director and the leader of a foundation that funds 50 percent of your operating budget comes to ask how it is doing. You're not going to feel terribly comfortable sharing negative feedback. The risks are too high. So for you, more than for most nonprofit programs, it's important to seriously consider using an external consultant—at least for the grantee facing data collection. Even through external consultants, it can still be hard for grantees to feel safe giving direct feedback to foundations.

And because of this dynamic, I strongly recommend that you find an evaluator who has experience with foundation evaluation. In general, I do not believe that external evaluators need expertise in your exact content area. Evaluators are there to bring the evaluation expertise and learn from you and your partners about the content area. But in the foundation context, using an evaluator that has lived through the foundation versus grantee dynamic and developed tips and tricks to minimize its effect is critical. Let's discuss involving grantees in evaluation.

Involving Grantees in the Evaluation Process

The last tip for evaluating the foundation is to consider whether and how you could engage grantees in the evaluation process—beyond using them as a data source. More and more frequently, I am seeing foundations convene a grantee advisory committee to help define the focus of the evaluation. This approach helps ensure alignment between the foundation's evaluation efforts and the role that grantees see the foundation playing in the community. This practice has the additional benefits of strengthening relationships with a subset of grantees, building evaluation capacity, and continuously educating the foundation about the changing needs and priorities of grantees.

Also, consider how you can involve grantees in the reflection and learning process like we discussed in **Chapter Seven.** Even if grantees are not involved in the initial design and focus, can you engage them in interpreting the results? My team has had great success with presenting findings to grantees, asking them for help with "Now What?" action planning, and developing specific recommendations for the foundation to address findings.

I've also seen more and more foundations making their evaluation results public, either focused on their work or on the work of their grantees. Addtionally, these foundations host a special sharing session to make sure grantees hear the findings first. According to a 2017 Foundation Center survey, only 55 percent of foundations currently share their evaluation findings externally, so this is an easy way to set your foundation apart. Now we are going to turn to the other side of foundation evaluation: evaluating the impact of your grantees.

Evaluating the Impact of Your Grantees

The other half of foundation evaluation is evaluating the impact of the foundation on the community. How do we know that the foundation is making a difference by funding in a specific area? Originally, evaluation was focused narrowly on individual programs or nonprofits. But since the late 1990s to the early 2000s, foundations have started experimenting with using evaluation to assess their philanthropic efforts. I have worked in philanthropic evaluation since the beginning of my career.

I started my journey in evaluation working for the Colorado Health Foundation and supporting its initial efforts around evaluation. And philanthropic evaluation continues to be a large portion of the work I do. At Vantage Evaluation, we regularly work with small and large, local and national foundations to help them develop an evaluation strategy or to evaluate a specific body of work. After a decade in philanthropic evaluation, I still believe that using evaluation in philanthropy is possible and important. But it's hard. Really hard. There are two main challenges of philanthropic evaluation:

The First Challenge: Indirect

First, foundation impact is almost entirely indirect. You are not directly touching the communities you serve. You are putting resources into the nonprofits that touch the communities. But your potential impact goes through the huge unknown of your grantees. You cannot make an impact unless your grantees make an impact. While you can control who you are dedicating resources to, you have limited control over what they do and how well they do it.

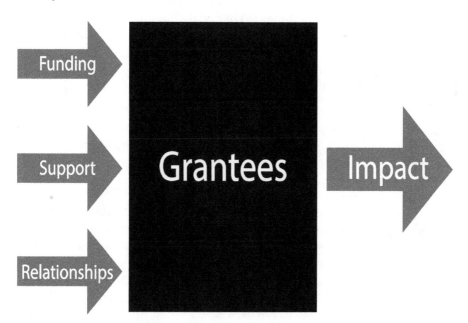

Then, even if you do discover an impact, how much of that can the foundation take credit for? If the foundation's work only has an impact through the work of grantees, is the foundation making a difference or are the grantees making a difference? For larger foundations that fund in very specific areas, the attribution of impact issue is smaller. They fund such a large percentage of work in a particular area that both they and their nonprofit partners are typically comfortable concluding that the impact would not have happened without the foundation, or at least that the foundation made a significant contribution to the impact.

But for smaller foundations and foundations that fund in diverse areas, nonprofit reliance on your dollars is lower and your ability to claim a significant portion of impact is more suspect. If you fall in the latter category, I'd strongly recommend that you target your evaluation dollars toward evaluating yourself or helping individual grantees beef up their strategies, instead of trying to design an evaluation strategy to capture your overall impact in the community.

The Second Challenge: Dependency

The second prominent challenge in philanthropy evaluation is that your evaluation work will only ever be as good as your grantees' evaluation work. Regardless of the evaluation approach a foundation takes, the foundation will always remain dependent on data from grantees. Whether the foundation is asking grantees to share data directly with the foundation or hiring an external evaluator to collect data from grantees, the quality of that data is still limited by grantees' evaluation capacity, particularly their processes and systems for collecting data.

In the face of the nonprofit capacity challenge, I contend that investing in foundation evaluation strategies is an uphill battle unless you also invest in building the evaluation capacity of your grantees. And strengthening grantee capacity must happen either simultaneously or, preferably, before building a foundation evaluation strategy for it to have a chance of success. Don't wait for someone else to do it—support your grantees in building the evaluation capacity that you expect of them.

Grantee Evaluation Capacity Remains Extremely Limited

According to the 2016 State of Evaluation, while over 90 percent of nonprofits nationally report using some form of evaluation, the quality is limited. Only 28 percent of those nonprofits exhibiting "promising" evaluation capacity have "some internal evaluation capacity, the existence of some foundational evaluation tools, and a practice of at least annually engaging in evaluation." The same study investigated barriers to evaluation among nonprofits and found the top challenges were limited staff time, insufficient financial resources, and limited staff knowledge, skills, and tools.

If you are still reading, I'm going to assume that you're not discouraged by the challenges of indirect impact and grantee evaluation capacity, and you're ready to jump in and start developing or revising an evaluation approach for your foundation. I'm glad. It can be done and when it is done well, it can make all the difference for a nonprofit community. Healthy Huerfano, the nonprofit we met at the beginning of this chapter, faced these challenges head-on. Together with her board, Maria decided to let go of the idea of claiming an impact. Recognizing that the impact of Healthy Huerfano necessarily goes through grantee partners, she designed its evaluation materials to specify its focus on the impact of grantees, supported by the foundation.

Maria does recognize that in a small community, Healthy Huerfano contributed to the impact, but does not claim the full impact. Additionally, the board approved the addition of evaluation to their existing capacity building funding stream to support the development of evaluation skills and systems in grantees. By addressing these challenges directly and publicly, Healthy Huerfano has experienced less push back and more respect and support from its nonprofit community than I typically see. While its evaluation work is still young, I am optimistic that over time this approach will produce more useful and authentic evaluation conversations as a community instead of just internally at the foundation.

Getting Started

So, how can you get started? There are four dominant approaches to foundation evaluation, shown on the continuum below. The approaches on the right are not "better" than the approaches on the left; the approaches on the right cover a greater breadth of foundation work. Additionally, these approaches are not mutually exclusive. The foundations that are known for their investments in evaluation, like the Hewlett Foundation, the Robert Wood Johnson Foundation, and the Kellogg Foundation, typically use *all four approaches*. You may only have capacity for one to start with, but they combine nicely when and if you grow the capacity to add more approaches.

In the remainder of this section, I present details about each approach, and then we close the chapter with a discussion about how foundations can

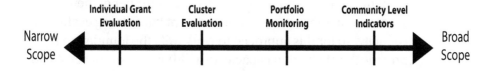

communicate about evaluation most effectively. Let's begin with individual grant evaluation and its pros and cons:

Individual Grant Evaluation

Individual grant evaluation focuses on evaluating each individual grant. Instead of trying to look at the impact of the foundation across a group or portfolio of grants, this approach treats each grant or each grantee individually and evaluates the impact of that one grant on the community.

The benefits of this approach are:

◆ It produces very tangible evaluation findings. The evaluation does not have to apply across disparate program activities, just this one program. Because it can focus so specifically on one grant or grantee, the evaluation looks more like traditional program evaluation.

◆ It creates good content for case studies that can bring evaluation to life for other grantees. Your communication team will be a strong partner in this approach.

◆ It is narrowly focused on one grantee, so it tends to highlight more actionable information for improvement than the more generalized approaches.

The downsides to individual grant evaluation:

◆ It's hard to know whether lessons you learn through this evaluation approach are generalizable because it focuses so narrowly on one grant or grantee.

◆ It can be viewed as irrelevant by other grantees if the work doesn't closely relate to what they are doing. Sharing lessons can be tricky because other grantees might push back on the differences between that grant or grantee and their work.

◆ It can get quite resource-intensive because foundations will sometimes try this approach with a large number of their grants. Remember, most grantees do not have strong evaluation capacity, so for this approach to work well, the foundation must provide the evaluation capacity usually via an external evaluator.

Be realistic about how many grantees you can afford to evaluate in depth each year.

So When Is Individual Grant Evaluation Recommended?

Individual grant evaluation is not the right approach for every organization. However, it may be the right approach for you if you are new to evaluation and have a subset of grantees uniquely significant to your work.

Just Getting Started

First, this approach is great if you are just getting started with evaluation and need to build internal support for evaluation. This approach is not disruptive to the rest of the foundation's work—it does not change how program officers are expected to do their work or require the development of any new internal systems. And when done well, I have seen this approach build a hunger for more evaluation: foundation staff and board see how much they learn from a grantee or two, and they want to know more about their other grantees.

Grantees Are Key to Your Work

Second, this approach is great when a subset of grantees are key to your work. Grantees might be key because they receive a level of funding significantly above most other grantees or when their work is central to your mission and goals. In that case, it can make more sense to target your evaluation resources selectively to those grantees than to distribute resource across your full portfolio. Third, this approach works well when the foundation is considering expanding into a new area. If you have the opportunity to fund a few grants in a new area, and then invest in individual grant evaluation for those grants, you can get a sense of what works and what doesn't before making more substantial, broad investments.

Cluster Evaluation

Cluster evaluation groups similar grants and then evaluates that group of grants. Some foundations group clusters by the program area, such as health-care grantees, or approach like integrating behavioral health into primary care clinics. Other foundations group clusters by geographic region. For instance, all grants to the Denver-metro region. And others group clusters by target population, such as native Spanish speakers.

The benefits of cluster evaluation are:

◆ Focus on learning and improving: Compared to portfolio monitoring, this approach pools grantees with some built-in similarities. As a result, it is well positioned to focus on learning and improving. If the evaluation findings are shared with grantees as they emerge, they can help both the foundation and the grantees learn from one another and improve their programs along the way.

◆ Results are generalizable: Compared to individual grant monitoring, this approach is more generalizable because it looks at multiple projects instead of one grantee. When the cluster is set narrowly enough, it can cull actionable lessons learned across a specific area.

◆ Grantees are inclined to share: Cluster evaluation can create connections between similar grantees, encouraging them to share and learn from one another.

◆ Consistency due to foundation involvement: Because cluster evaluations are commissioned by the foundation, the foundation retains control over the focus and approach to evaluation. The cluster approach is unlike the other three approaches, which are more reliant on the grantee's evaluation perspective, such as individual grant evaluation and portfolio monitoring, or the secondary data source like communitylevel indicators.

The downsides to cluster evaluation are:

◆ Limited pool of grantees: For foundations that fund in multiple areas, this approach captures only a subset of grantees. You can build out a cluster evaluation for each of your focus areas, but of course, that multiplies the resources required.

◆ Heavily reliant on external evaluators: Even foundations that have an internal evaluation function commission cluster evaluations.

◆ Dependent on staff time: Foundations without an internal evaluation function must be sure that there is a staff member dedicated to managing and guiding the cluster evaluation contract. Even when using an external contractor, the foundation must remain involved in setting the direction and maintaining relationships with grantees, or the end product will diverge from the foundation's needs.

◆ Risk associated with narrowly defining the cluster: If the cluster is not defined narrowly enough, the evaluation will deteriorate to "lowest common denominator" evaluation, capturing the things that the grants have in common even if they are not the most important things. For example, if you fund health access work but the grantees in that area run very different programs, meaning one provides transportation to medical services while another embeds behavioral health providers in clinics, then doing a "health access" cluster is not a great idea. Instead, consider clustering by strategy. For example, look at all the grants that provide transportation to medical services.

So When Is Cluster Evaluation Recommended?

If you have adequate resources and time, you may choose cluster evaluations to evaluate grantees who are working on a significant grant, either in terms of funding or focus area.

The Foundation Has Discreet Granting Pools

First and foremost, this approach is best when the foundation has clear, consistent, and constrained buckets of grants. This is the essential condition for cluster evaluation. Second, I see this approach most often for foundations that have a "signature" focus area and want a strong understanding of what is happening in that area. For example, a foundation might broadly focus on health care but has a unique and high-profile portfolio of grants to improve dental care. That portfolio is a good

The Foundation Wants to Evaluate After the Fact

Occasionally, foundations that want to do a cluster evaluation after the fact, perhaps for grants over the previous three years, approach me. But when those grants were awarded, the foundation did not establish the expectation that the grantees would be asked to participate in evaluation. So then when the evaluator comes in, the grantees do not have the bandwidth nor the buy-in to participate. Grantees rarely actively protest, because maintaining a positive relationship with the foundation is in their best interest, but the passive resistance to the evaluator can negatively impact the quality of the end product. Avoid this outcome by building in cluster evaluation from the start. Set participation expectations with grantees at the time of their award and provide additional funding to support the bandwidth required to participate.

Portfolio Evaluation Rarely Lives Up to Expectations

In practice, portfolio monitoring rarely lives up to expectations. Most of the foundations that started with portfolio monitoring as their core evaluation approach have since prioritized more substantive cluster or individual grant evaluation approaches, including the Colorado Health Foundation.

candidate for cluster evaluation. Third, this approach works well for foundations that are able to build evaluation requirements and funding support into the initial grant contract.

Portfolio Monitoring

Portfolio monitoring identifies a set of indicators and asks all grantees in the portfolio to collect and report data on that set of indicators. For some foundations, that means having a small number of indicators and asking every grantee to report all indicators. For others, it means having a large number of indicators and asking each grantee to report on a subset. When I started at the Colorado Health Foundation in 2009, this was the evaluation approach I was charged with helping to build out. The Colorado Health Foundation had identified twelve measurable results and when the grant was awarded, the program officer identified one or more to include in the grant contract.

The Downsides to Portfolio Monitoring

Portfolio monitoring is an insufficient tool for many foundations due to its limitations.

The Lowest Common Denominator

Portfolio monitoring necessarily becomes the "lowest common denominator" evaluation for the reasons that we talked about in the previous section. When you are looking at indicators across a broad range of grantee nonprofits and program types, most foundations end up capturing superficial "output" numbers, like the number of people served by program. In an effort to create consistency, the approach misses indicators that could speak more directly to the impact of participation in those programs.

No Information for Improvement

Portfolio monitoring does not provide any information for improvement without additional data. At the Colorado Health Foundation, I would review grantees to find trends about which nonprofits were able to achieve more and why. Occasionally, we would find an insight, but more often we would find differences in performance without any evidence of why. Portfolio monitoring without a supplemental approach to understand the why and how behind the numbers remains limited in its ability to uncover insights and drive program improvement.

Relies Entirely on the Evaluation Capacity of Grantees

I have never seen an effective "check" for whether the grantees actually have the capacity to report the indicators. Of course, program officers ask. And understandably, nonprofits say, "Yes, of course!" since they want the funding. But on the back-end, there is no verification that the grantee has systems to capture this information. For example, I commonly worked on grants where the program staff reported they would serve 2,500 individuals through the course of the grant. In comes the report, and wouldn't you know it, the program served *exactly* 2,500 individuals that year! Really?

So When Is Portfolio Monitoring Recommended?

Despite the limitations, portfolio monitoring is still a good option in certain situations that require time and a capacity for communication and oversight.

When the Funding Focus Is Narrow

This approach works best in foundations that have a very narrow funding focus. Think about cases when consistent indicators would actually make good sense because all the funded programs are so similar.

When You're Building Grantee Capacity

This approach works well when the foundation dedicates resources to building the evaluation capacity of grantees to report on the mandated indicators. Consider ways to support grantees upfront and also ways to "audit." Trust but verify (!) the numbers grantees report at the end of the grant.

When You Can Offer Strong Communications

Portfolio monitoring approaches require strong communications campaigns to help grantees understand that the evaluation is for learning and growth, not punishing them for unmet goals. Part of the reason I've read so many "We said we'd serve 2,500 and we did serve 2,500!" grant reports is capacity, but the other root cause is fear. Grantees are willing to gamble that they are less likely to get called out on bogus numbers than they are to lose funding if they report not-so-great actual numbers. Especially when the foundation does not have the evaluation capacity to follow up on suspect numbers.

Community-Level Indicators

The last evaluation approach common in foundation evaluation is monitoring changes in community-level indicators. For example, a health foundation might monitor the obesity rate in a community and use a decrease as evidence that its work has been successful.

The benefits of community-level indicators are few. Like portfolio monitoring, the benefits on this approach are mostly theoretical, with very real downsides:

◆ Like portfolio monitoring, this approach feels tangible and like the most exact measure of a foundation's entire impact.

◆ It represents the long-term end goal of a foundation's work that we are all working to capture.

◆ You're trying to change the community, so why not measure your success by how much the community changes? Well, because of the limitations below.

Community-Level Indicator Evaluation Downsides

The downsides of community-level indicator evaluation are numerous. I've listed some of the most common reasons below.

There Are Too Many Factors

There are too many other factors to impact community-level indicators for your foundation to claim credit for improvement or responsibility for worsening. Your foundation's dollars is only one input into a complicated system. Take the obesity rate, for example. Obesity is impacted by genetics, community culture, parenting, trauma, poverty, food access, physical activity access, education and awareness, grocery store openings and closings, city infrastructure like sidewalks and playgrounds, weather, etc., etc., etc. How much of that can your foundation actually change?

Foundations Are Drawn to Using Ranking Data For the Wrong Reasons

Often foundations are drawn to using ranking data to say that they are the "healthiest" or "most educated" community in a state or state in the nation.

Rankings further compound the issue of confounding factors. In addition to considering all the factors that impact your obesity rate, you also have to consider what impacts the obesity rate in other communities. You could do the most effective obesity reduction work in the world, but what if someone else does too? If your obesity rate decreases by 3 percent but another community's decreases by 4 percent, is that a failure?

It Takes a Long Time to See a Change in a Community-Level Indicator

Consider something like early childcare funding. You might look at indicators like educational attainment, health outcomes, or third-grade reading proficiency. Even the soonest indicator, third-grade reading proficiency, is *five to six years* removed from a three-year-old participating in an early childhood program. That's a long time to wait to see if a program works. And then think about how much happens to kids in the five to six years that might also influence third-grade reading proficiency.

Reliance on Others

This approach is reliant on data that someone else collects, so it may not be exactly what you are hoping to measure. One of the most common challenges with secondary data is that the information is collapsed, rather than separated by category. For example, you may want facts about access to public parks, when all you can find are figures that combine access to parks, playgrounds, and libraries. Another hurdle you may encounter occurs when you're seeking statistics about a specific timeline. Say you want to track progress every three years, when the secondary data only reports every five years. Yet another common challenge happens when you need information about a specific geographic area, when the only available data is split into two different census tracts that include unwanted neighboring areas.

Inadequate Information

And lastly, like portfolio monitoring, community health indicators alone don't give you adequate information about why a change happened. So the obesity rate does decrease—what, of all the strategies your foundation used, drove that decrease the most? If you don't know that, how do you continue or expand the right body of work? Let's understand this approach further by looking at an example in the next passage.

When Is This Approach Recommended?

I don't ever recommend using community-level indicators as your only evaluation method. In fact, I advocate against it. Community-level

How Does the Huerfano Story End?

Now that I've gone over the four common approaches for foundation evaluation, I bet you're wondering: what did Healthy Huerfano end up doing? Well, like most foundations I work with, it chose a combination of approaches. The evaluation model in the first year used cluster evaluation to focus on a specific funding area, portfolio monitoring to track target population across all grants, and community-level indicators to track health outcomes and community needs. In the second year, it continued portfolio monitoring and community-level indicators, used cluster evaluation with a different group of grantees, and also added individual grant evaluation for two core grantees and capacity building funding to support grantees' own evaluation work.

	Pros	Cons	When to Use
Individual Grant Evaluation	◆ Tangible ◆ Demonstrates the power of evaluation ◆ Actionable	◆ Generalizability ◆ Relevance to other grantees ◆ Resource intensity at scale	◆ Just getting started with evaluation ◆ Key subset of grantees ◆ Consideration of new funding area
Cluster Evaluation	◆ Learning-oriented ◆ More generalizable ◆ Connections between grantees ◆ Control	◆ Only a subset of grants ◆ Reliance on external evaluators ◆ Staff manager of external evaluators ◆ Defining the cluster narrowly enough	◆ Clear, constrained funding buckets ◆ "Signature" funding areas ◆ Evaluation built in from the start of the grant

Portfolio Monitoring	◆ Covers full portfolio of grantees ◆ Appealing to boards and executives	◆ "Lowest common denominator" ◆ No information to drive improvement ◆ Limited grantee evaluation capacity	◆ Very narrow funding focus ◆ Dedicated resources to capacity building ◆ Strong communication with grantees
Community-Level Indicators	◆ Tangible ◆ Most "direct" measure of end-goal impact	◆ Other influencing factors in your community ◆ For ranking data: other influencing factors in other communities ◆ Long timeline ◆ Limitations of secondary data ◆ No information	◆ As a supplement to other approaches ◆ The largest funder in a narrow focus area in a targeted region

indicators make a great supplement to other evaluation strategies if, and only if, you are the largest foundation in a narrowly targeted geographic region with a narrowly targeted focus area. For example, the Bill and Melinda Gates Foundation is by far the largest funder of malaria vaccination programs in Africa, with billions of dollars invested since 1999. In this case, monitoring vaccination rates and malaria rates make sense. In fact, Bill and Melinda Gates Foundation is able to compare vaccination and malaria rates in different African countries where different strategies have been taken, and in that way have the rare experience of gaining actionable strategy insights from community-level indicators.

Before we end the chapter, it's critical that we talk about how to communicate about evaluation with your grantees. Remember, the foundation or grantee power dynamic impacts evaluation too.

Communicating about Evaluation

As a foundation, everything you do has trickle-down effects on the grantees you support, supported, or might support in the future. Even the rumor that a foundation might change funding priorities or approaches can send waves of fear throughout a nonprofit community. This is not new information to you—this is the reality of the foundation-grantee relationship that you live in every day. And yet, there is still a risk in the way that added or expanded evaluation work is presented to grantees: your excitement about the power of evaluation will blind you to grantee anxiety and misunderstanding.

Let's go a little bit deeper into what I'm talking about. Hopefully, by the time you have finished this book, you'll be ready to go with evaluation. You're all-in on the value of evaluation to nonprofits and foundations and ready to proceed full speed ahead in adding or expanding your evaluation efforts. And often that excitement can make you forget your former evaluation anxiety and misunderstanding. Because the majority of the evaluation messages that nonprofits receive are still of the "rigorous research design" for "judgment and accountability" flavors, those of us who see a different future for evaluation have to constantly temper our excitement with a recognition of the mindset in the rest of the community. For more details about the more typical evaluation message, return to **Part One**.

You will have to lead your grantees on the journey you went through in this book. Hand-in-hand with an added or expanded evaluation strategy must come extensive grantee education and reassurance. Because, if you just say "evaluation," grantees will hear "punitive." So share your understanding of the power of evaluation. Share your approach to evaluation as a learning tool, where both grantees and the foundation are learning toward the same goals. Reiterate again and again that funding will not be cut for poor results but might be if the nonprofit doesn't attempt to learn from poor results. Share your perspective that evaluation should be tailored to each nonprofit's information needs—and empower grantees to develop their own evaluation practices. And share your intentions to close feedback loops by distributing results and learnings with them.

Don't expect one round of education and reassurance to be enough. It takes time and repetition to change mindsets, and your evaluation approach will only be successful if grantees are on board. Even passive resistance from grantees can lead a foundation to evaluation based on faulty data because at the end of the day, a foundation's evaluation relies on the strength of its grantees' evaluation.

I share this last piece of advice with you not to discourage you from proceeding with evaluation, but to set the stage for the reality I've seen play out in practice. Healthy Huerfano fell into this exact sticky situation with its early evaluation efforts. Staff got so excited so fast once they recognized the potential of what evaluation could add to their nonprofit, they immediately started sharing that excitement out in the community. Not through any formal announcement, but just the "excitement is seeping out of me, and I can't contain it" causal conversations that happen in any small community. And as a result, its grantees panicked. One grantee told another that Healthy Huerfano was talking about evaluation, and through the rumor mill, that quickly became that Healthy Huerfano was mandating extensive evaluation in its next grant round.

To its credit, Healthy Huerfano was close enough to the community to notice this happening and quickly addressed it. The foundation staff scheduled a series of educational events on evaluation, sharing why they were excited, what their approach would be, and what that did and did not mean for grantees. Grantees calmed down and actively participated in the first year of evaluation. Then Healthy Huerfano practiced what it preached by sharing the evaluation findings with the community and looking to its grantees for ideas and changes in response to the findings.

At this point, I hope you've found a few useful tips to strengthen how you, as a foundation, engage in evaluation. What one thing can you take away and immediately implement in your nonprofit? Hand this book and your evaluation commitment off to the executive director of the nonprofit who shared it with you.

Part Four

Let's Get Started

Each of the pieces we've covered up to this point come together to transform a nonprofit. In **Part One**, we set the stage for why a repositioning of evaluation was necessary. In **Part Two**, we outlined the process to make evaluation as learning a reality. In **Part Three,** we went position by position through a nonprofit to support each staff role's engagement with evaluation. Now in **Part Four,** we bring it all together with a summary of how the puzzle pieces fit together in **Chapter Thirteen,** and how to take the first step in **Chapter Fourteen.**

Chapter Thirteen

Bringing It All Together

In this chapter, let's draw the connections between all of the pieces we've talked about so far. First, we share how the evaluation steps in **Part Two** and the contribution of each position in **Part Three** combine to create forward progress with evaluation efforts. Second, we highlight the major themes that emerge throughout the book. By holding the big picture in mind, it's easier to see how each small step in the next chapter represents progress and forward motion, even when there is more work to be done. How do these pieces fit together? The best analogy for how each of the preceding chapters fit together is human anatomy.

The Body of Evaluation

The five steps of evaluation from **Part Two** create the spine that frames and guides evaluation efforts. Without those five steps, the evaluation is flimsy, missing critical supports, and incapable of producing meaningful evaluation consistently. The five positions form the head and the limbs. The executive director is the head, with a big picture view of where evaluation efforts need to go and control over the movement of the arms and legs. The development

staff and communications staff make up the arms, able to implement the vision of the executive director and structure of the spine by picking up support for evaluation and handing out evaluation findings. And the board and funders make up the legs, providing a foundational base of support for evaluation efforts.

Without all ten elements moving in the same direction, you won't make any progress. And yet, a weakness in one limb is not fatal—it can be supplemented by strength in the others. What does it look like when all the parts are in place?

Evaluation Steps Lead to Movement

When all ten of these elements come together, nonprofits look fundamentally different. They can have strategic conversations about less-than-perfect evaluation results with staff and board without defensiveness. They can incorporate changes while protecting the program's secret sauce. And they can advocate for the human and financial capacity they need for meaningful evaluation. Let's return to a nonprofit I introduced in **Chapter Ten,** Books for All.

Books for All

In our first introduction to Books for All, we focused on Tori, a member of the development team who was an active participant in evaluation efforts. But the truth is, everyone on Books for All's staff is engaged in the evaluation. The initial meeting to map the program and articulate key evaluation questions included program staff, development staff, the VP of communications, and the executive director. The evaluation approach and design were shared with and approved by the board, and directly funded by foundation partners. The entire program team was engaged in supporting data collection throughout the year. And the process of reflecting on results again included staff from across the nonprofit in programs, development, communication, and leadership. The results discussion was open to all staff, and one of the most engaged participants was a new junior back-office staff member.

Not all of the results have been positive, and Books for All has shared the mixed results honestly with funders, along with plan for what it is going to do about it. Despite significant staff turnover during our partnership, Books for All remains committed to using evaluation as a core strategic tool. And I see that commitment play out in everyday actions. Staff comb through evaluation results and use them throughout the year to make strategic tweaks. They change their evaluation annually to pursue new questions. They push back on funders' evaluation requirements, and in some cases let go of funding that does not support their evaluation approach. Evaluation makes a regular appearance in marketing and communications materials. And they talk about evaluation as a learning process at all levels of the nonprofit, including program staff, the leadership team, with the board of directors, and with major donors. I am often asked to identify nonprofits that model exceptional evaluation practices, and Books for All is at the top of my list. It is not about having perfect evaluation results. It is about a nonprofit coming together to engage with and learn from evaluation over time.

Why Isn't There a Chapter for Program Staff?

I went back and forth on whether to include a chapter specifically for program staff in this book. Ultimately, I decided not to. This decision is not indicative of the lack of importance of program staff in evaluation efforts. In fact, the reality is the opposite: program staff are so key to successful evaluation efforts that they need the support in this entire book, not a single chapter. If you think about evaluation as part of program work, then all of **Part Two** is the chapter for program staff. In most of the nonprofits I work with, the program staff play a leading role in guiding and managing the evaluation. Often, they are the impetus for starting evaluation efforts, the manager of any external evaluation partner, and the deciding voice for program changes as a result of evaluation findings. If you think about our evaluation anatomy, program staff are the veins, arteries, and nerves that flow through it all.

Major Themes Across the Evaluation Anatomy

This book is filled with tips and strategies to help improve your evaluation efforts. It may seem like a lot of disparate pieces, but they all emerge from the same core themes and perspective. I could summarize the entire book in five points:

Don't Do the Math

Evaluation is not about technical skills and math, it is a thought process that any nonprofit staff can engage in to make their work more effective. Sometimes when I ask people why they dislike evaluation, they respond "Oh, I'm not a math person." But how many times in this book did we talk about math? While there are elements of evaluation that require some math, the fundamental processes of evaluation require none. Instead, evaluation requires thinking and reflection that any critical mind can do.

Learn to Adapt

The purpose of evaluation is to learn and to improve, not to hold accountable. Evaluation as a tool for some external entity to hold nonprofits accountable to what they said they would do has done far more harm

When we look at the evaluation anatomy and the themes across each body part, we can find some clarity in how nonprofits can help overcome the challenges of the evaluation field outlined in **Part One**. How about a "Nonprofit Evaluation Bill of Rights," specifying what you should expect in your evaluation work?

Nonprofit Evaluation Bill of Rights

1. *You have a right to determine the focus of your evaluation.*

Never again should your evaluation direction be driven by funders or your evaluator. Your learning priorities are the most important needs and should be the core focus of your evaluation. Start there, then add bits onto the edges to address reporting requirements.

2. *You have a right to an evaluator with the technical skills to get the work done and the ability to communicate the work so that you can understand it.*

Evaluators, whether on your staff or an external partner, should speak your language instead of expecting you to learn theirs. Don't pay for a product that you can't understand.

3. *You have a right to not have your evaluation results used against you.*

Evaluation is a learning journey, and imperfect results don't automatically mean the program should be canceled. Push back on those who want to hold you accountable for imperfect results with a plan for how the results can help make your programming better.

4. *You have a right to ask for financial resources to support your evaluation.*

Evaluation takes time, money, and capacity. Use your clarity on the importance of evaluation to support ongoing improvement and to advocate for evaluation funding. And if you don't have adequate financial resources to support evaluation, reconsider doing it. Under-resourced evaluation can be worse for a nonprofit than no evaluation.

than good. At its best, evaluation helps nonprofits learn more about their programs and services so they can make improvements and better serve our communities. What makes a nonprofit effective is not having positive evaluation results but being able to adapt and tweak in response to both positive and negative evaluation results. Because the world is not static and what works this year won't work in five years.

Where Evaluation Begins

If evaluation is in service of learning and improving, it must be driven by the program. The days of external stakeholders driving the focus on evaluation have passed. What do you need to know to do your job better? That is where evaluation should start. Funder reporting requirements are not going to go away, but they should be secondary in the evaluation priority list, not primary. And this transition requires a change in both nonprofits and funders. Nonprofits, it is on you to advocate for the evaluation that makes sense for your organization. And funders, it is on you to listen and help adapt your reporting requirements to nonprofits' intentional evaluation efforts.

Don't Rinse and Repeat

Evaluation should not repeat ad nauseum. There are very few evaluations that make sense to repeat exactly year after year. If you articulate key evaluation questions, then answer those questions. Good questions should generate new questions and the evaluation should evolve to match. Some questions need multiple years to answer, but each year you should get a little closer and the evaluation should change to add new information to the picture each year.

Work in Teams

And lastly, evaluation is a team sport. It does not live nicely in one staff person's bucket. Instead, evaluation works only when it is woven into the fabric of the nonprofit across staff roles. Yes, someone needs to own evaluation and make sure it gets done. But it takes the engagement of the full team for evaluation to deliver its full value. You never know where insights will come from, and having each role engaged in the articulation of key evaluation questions and interpretation of evaluation findings maximizes the chance that you have the full picture.

Chapter Fourteen

Taking the First Step

We've covered a lot of ground in this book. You might be overwhelmed with the work ahead of you or excited about the possibilities! Regardless of how you feel, know that you've accomplished the first step in your journey toward using evaluation as a learning process: you've read this book. But what's the second step? How do you narrow down all of the suggestions in this book to a reasonable to-do list that you can tackle successfully? There are three options for you to consider: First, to start with whatever sings to you. Second, proceed in the order of each section, going chapter by chapter and implementing the full process. Third, use my list of top ten highest evaluation leverage points to narrow your list.

Option One: Pick Your Own Adventure

This book is full of tips and immediately actionable strategies. And I sincerely believe that nonprofits are best off with starting with whatever resonates most with their staff. There is not one most important step; rather, the most important step is the first one you take. The bar for evaluation in most nonprofits is so low that any improvement, especially the early changes, can make a huge difference. Option one is to start with whatever tip, anywhere in this book, is most compelling to you. Then once you have implemented that, pick the next, and so on and so on, not stopping until evaluation takes hold and becomes an indispensable strategic tool in your work.

Option Two: Chapter by Chapter

The structure of this book is not a mistake. Each of the five chapters in **Part Two** build off of the previous to add depth to your evaluation process. The positions in **Part Three** are in the order that I've found most critical to build an awareness and understanding of evaluation. Option two is to follow the structure of the sections in this book, ideally with **Part Two** and **Part Three** proceeding simultaneously. Engage your team in the evaluation planning process in **Chapters Three** through **Five,** in that order. Then move on to implementing the evaluation as described in **Chapter Six** and with the support of outside details on each method you select. Then you can try suggestions to reflect and learn in **Chapter Seven.**

All along the way, your team should be using the guidance in their positional chapter from **Part Three** to support and enhance the evaluation process. Some roles come into play earlier, like the development staff advocating for increased evaluation funding. And some come later, like the communication staff publicizing the evaluation findings. So it's important to utilize **Part Three** simultaneously with **Part Two,** instead of sequentially. And when you are done with **Chapter Seven,** start over from the beginning. Evaluation is not a one-time effort, and my team and I find the second round is where the magic happens. At that point, the process and the mindset is not new, and the staff are all the more engaged after experiencing some early evaluation wins.

Option Three: Elena's Top Ten

To some of you, option one may seem too chaotic and option two too extensive. Option Three is the Goldilocks of starting points: more directive than starting wherever you want, but narrower than doing everything. Based on my experience as both an internal and external evaluator, I believe that these ten changes have the highest evaluation leverage. Each has a high bang for the buck, changing the nonprofit's relationship with evaluation more than the work required. You need not implement these in the order in which they are presented: some are easy and quick while others are longer-term culture change. Instead, view this as your "short list" from which to pick your own starting place:

1. Use Key Evaluation Questions to Focus Your Evaluation (Chapter Four)

If I were queen of the universe, every nonprofit would have key evaluation questions and would use them to guide their evaluation. When evaluation is used as a learning process, it is key evaluation questions that set the focus and direction of the evaluation. The process of developing key evaluation questions engages staff across the nonprofit and resets the expectation that evaluation should serve a useful purpose. In my experience, key evaluation questions are the *sine qua non* of useful evaluation and the early win that positions evaluation efforts for success. Nonprofits with whom I've done years of evaluation work to this day still identify the process of developing key evaluation questions as the most impactful element of our partnership. If you ask me where to start, I'd say start with key evaluation questions.

2. Advocate for Adequate Evaluation Funding (Chapters Six, Eight, Ten, and Twelve)

After you have key evaluation questions, use them to advocate for the funding you need to find the answers. My hope is that after reading this book, you will never again accept evaluation as an unfunded grant requirement. If every reader pushes back on funders to support the evaluation that grants request, the tides will turn. A major theme of this book is that useful evaluation takes time, money, and staff commitment. And that when those investments are adequate for the questions at hand, evaluation yields invaluable insights that improve programs and services and, in turn, transform our communities. Funders share that commitment to the community and should contribute financially to evaluation as a key element of effective nonprofit work.

3. Banish Accountability from Your Vocabulary (Chapters One and Seven)

Evaluation is described in this book as a learning process to support strategic programming and only works when consistently positioned in that way. Every time evaluation is conveyed as an accountability measure, it sets the evaluation efforts back. This is especially true among the nonprofit's leadership team and board of directors. The staff are sensitive to your words and your actions, so take special care to frame all evaluation conversations and tasks within in a frame of learning and improvement.

4. Recruit the Executive Director as a Champion (Chapter Eight)

The nonprofits that are most successful in their evaluation efforts are those where executive directors are vocal advocates for evaluation, even if they are not the impetus for the evaluation. If you are reading this book as a staff or board member, your number one job now is to recruit your executive director as a champion for evaluation. Just having a blessing is not sufficient. You need authentic commitment to evaluation as a learning process and willingness to put leadership and nonprofit capacity behind the effort. If you are reading this book as the executive director, your number one job is to use your position to prioritize evaluation efforts and weave them into the fabric of the nonprofit.

5. *Create a Shared Understanding Among Staff* (Chapter Two)

Everyone comes to evaluation with a different set of baggage and most of it is bad. For evaluation to stick in any nonprofit, every staff member needs a shared understanding of evaluation as a learning process and a shared language that focuses on the concepts and thought process, not the technical jargon. A single conversation is a good starting point, but insufficient. The best way I've found to get started is by resetting the playing field, then enabling staff to experience the power of evaluation learning for themselves by going through the process outlined in this book.

6. *Create a Shared Understanding Among the Board* (Chapter Eleven)

In addition to your staff, establishing a shared language for and understanding of evaluation on the board of directors is critical to the sustainability of evaluation efforts. Every time board members ask for an impact dashboard an evaluator winces. Help them understand what to ask for instead. Their involvement in the process is more confined than the staff members' roles, but regularly including evaluation on the board agenda and facilitating informative conversations helps them build their nonprofit muscles. It also increases the likelihood that evaluation will be embedded into the nonprofit's culture independent of any one champion.

7. *Consider Qualitative Data Sources* (Chapter Five)

In my experience, almost every nonprofit has an overemphasis on quantitative data. It's an unhelpful practice where evaluation is portrayed as accountability and when funders push for "quantifiable impact." This practice has served nonprofits poorly. Remember, understanding occurs in the overlap between quantitative and qualitative data sources. So how can you rebalance and incorporate meaningful sources of qualitative data to answer your key evaluation questions?

8. *Close your Feedback Loops* (Chapters Seven *and* Nine)

When nonprofits lament about low response rates to their evaluation, my first question is, "How do participants know that you value, hear, and use their feedback?" To which I receive blank stares. Sending informative thank-you notes, where you share what you learned and what you plan to do with participant feedback, is the number one strategy to increase participant engagement in evaluation. It is low-hanging fruit that improves any evaluation effort you have in place.

9. Structure the Presentation of Findings (Chapters Seven *and* Nine)

Another low-hanging fruit is the introduction of data sandwiches in the way you present evaluation findings to staff, board, funders, and external stakeholders. The idea that data should be presented in digestible packages that lead with a statement of what the data means is the most popular tip in my evaluation trainings. Again and again, I hear from trainees how much this change alone has transformed use of and engagement with evaluation findings.

10. Provide Opportunities to Reflect on Data at Least Annually (Chapter Seven)

I believe that much of the fear and skepticism about evaluation stems from a lack of opportunity to engage with the insights that emerge from evaluation. Data parties change that pattern in two ways: First, data parties provide an opportunity to pull data from different corners of the nonprofit into the same conversation. The staff person that manages student feedback might never talk to the staff person that manages teacher feedback, and yet insights hide in the intersection of these two sources. Second, data parties change evaluation from a passive activity—we receive a report, and maybe read it—to an active engagement. Staff members digest and interpret the findings and develop the action items instead of waiting for someone else to tell them what to do.

And with that, I will leave you to get started. I hope this book has framed evaluation in a way that serves you and your nonprofit as well as gives you evaluation tools to generate insights that help you do your job better.

Appendix A

Glossary

A/B Testing: A/B testing compares the performance of two or more versions of the same piece of content to determine which is more effective.

Center for Effective Philanthropy (CEP) Perception Reports: CEP has four proprietary assessment tools to measure grantee, applicant, donor, and staff perceptions of a foundation.

Color scripting: A feedback method where staff members ask attendees to fill out cards with one question at the event. Then cards are grouped by emotion back at the office (e.g., overwhelmed, excited, processing, etc.).

Commitment cards: A feedback method where attendees are asked to fill out cards stating one action they plan to take as a result of an event.

Data parties: Data parties follow a basic "What?—So What?—Now What?" structure, which guides the sharing of and discussion about your topic.

Data placemats: An example of a data party focusing on visually presenting key evaluation questions and the most critical data for each question. Space is available below the visual for participants to take notes.

Data sandwiches: A reporting format that has three parts: a conclusion, the supporting data, and a pretty picture.

Data vomit: A reporting style that takes random numbers and random words and throws them randomly on a grant report with no structure, logic, or flow.

Evaluation: The making of a judgment about the amount, number, or value of something.

Gallery walk: Adapted from teachers in a classroom, the gallery walk is an example of a data party, where participants are broken into small groups and rotate around each poster containing information for a fixed period of time.

Guessing game: An example of a data party that involves participants guessing what they think the results of the evaluation will be, which starts the conversation and centers the discussion around data.

Impact: Having a strong effect on someone or something.

Informative thank-you note: An evaluation tool that is actually communication with your beneficiary. It's an opportunity to share what you've learned and what you're planning to do with the information. It also includes a chance for the recipient to share additional feedback.

Key evaluation questions (KEQs): Help you specify why you want to do an evaluation at all and what you want to learn as a result of that evaluation. KEQs should focus on some aspect of the quality, worth, or significance of a program. KEQs should be evaluative, pertinent, reasonable, specific, and answerable.

Learning wall: A feedback method where attendees are prompted to post one piece of information or strategy they learned on a wall display.

Logic model: Graphically illustrate program components, helping you clearly identify program inputs and activities and the anticipated outcomes of the work.

Mini-interviews: A feedback method where staff members audio- or video-record attendees answer a single interview question as they move through an event.

Nonprofit Evaluation Bill of Rights: A list that specifies what you can and should expect in your evaluation work.

Objective: A thing aimed at or sought; a goal.

Outcomes: The way a thing turns out; a consequence.

Outputs: The amount of something produced by a person, machine, or industry.

Program evaluation standards: Utility, feasibility, propriety, and accuracy.

Program map: A clear articulation of what your program is trying to do, what your program does, and how those two things logically link.

Purpose statement: A two-sentence summary of why you want to do evaluation in the first place and what the results will be used for. It's a bit like a mission statement, but just for your evaluation.

Qualitative data: Explore a topic you know little about by capturing how and why answers.

Quantitative data: Precise, specific, concrete information that answer scale and scope questions.

Reasonable evaluation budget: The rule of thumb is that evaluation should be 10 percent of the program budget—not the grant budget—or $5,000, whichever is larger.

Research method: Quantitative or qualitative approaches to gathering information, such as surveys, tracking data, secondary data, focus groups, interview, and observations.

Structured observation: A feedback method where staff members use a tailored checklist to observe how attendees interact with components of an event and each other.

Suggestion wheel: A feedback method where attendees are asked what they would like to see more of, less of, stopped, started, and continued via a public display poster.

Theory of change: Graphically illustrate a causal path linking activities and outcomes and explaining how and why the desired outcomes are plausible.

Appendix B

Resources

Program Evaluation Standards:

http://www.jcsee.org/program-evaluation-standards-statements

American Evaluation Association Guiding Principles for Evaluators:

https://www.eval.org/p/cm/ld/fid=51

Best Resources for Surveys:

https://www.cdc.gov/healthyyouth/evaluation/pdf/brief15.pdf

https://www.cdc.gov/dhdsp/programs/spha/docs/constructing_survey_questions_tip_sheet.pdf

https://learningstore.uwex.edu/Assets/pdfs/G3658-14.pdf

Best Resources for Interviews and Focus Groups:

https://www.eiu.edu/ihec/Krueger-FocusGroupInterviews.pdf

https://ctb.ku.edu/en/table-of-contents/evaluate/evaluate-community-initiatives/interview-key-participants/main

http://toolkit.pellinstitute.org/evaluation-guide/analyze/analyze-qualitative-data

Best Resource for Observation:

https://www.cdc.gov/healthyyouth/evaluation/pdf/brief16.pdf

Best Resource for Program Tracking:

https://ctb.ku.edu/en/table-of-contents/evaluate/evaluate-community-initiatives/monitor-progress/main

Best Resource for Secondary Data Sources:

https://knowhownonprofit.org/organisation/impact/measuring-your-impact/secondary-data

Vantage Evaluation Resources (case studies, samples, blog, training calendar):

http://www.vantage-eval.com

Appendix C

Nonprofit Evaluation Bill of Rights

1. You have a right to determine the focus of your evaluation. Never again should your evaluation direction be driven by funders or your evaluator. Your learning priorities are the most important needs and should be the core focus of your evaluation. Start there, then add bits onto the edges to address reporting requirements.

2. You have a right to an evaluator with the technical skills to get the work done *and* the ability to communicate the work so that you can understand it. Evaluators, whether on your staff or an external partner, should speak your language instead of expecting you to learn theirs. Don't pay for a product that you can't understand.

3. You have a right to not have your evaluation results used against you. Evaluation is a learning journey, and imperfect results don't automatically mean the program should be canceled. Push back on those who want to hold you accountable for imperfect results with a plan for how the results can help make your programming better.

4. You have a right to ask for financial resources to support your evaluation. Evaluation takes time, money, and capacity. Use your clarity on the importance of evaluation to your ongoing improvement to advocate for funding to support evaluation. And if you don't have adequate financial resources to support evaluation, reconsider doing it. Under-resourced evaluation can be worse for a nonprofit than no evaluation.

Index

CPSIA information can be obtained
at www.ICGtesting.com
Printed in the USA
FSHW021302190119

9 781938 077920